THE D~~RAMATIC ARTS~~
AND CULTURAL STUDIES

LIBRARY

Tel: 01244 375444   Ext: 3301

CHESTER COLLEGE

This book is to be returned on or before the
last date stamped below. Overdue charges
will be incurred by the late return of books.

- 2 MAR 2004   - 1 APR 2006

- 8 APR 2005

1 6 NOV 2005

GARLAND REFERENCE LIBRARY OF SOCIAL SCIENCE
VOLUME 861

Teaching and Thinking
Shirley R. Steinberg and Joe L. Kincheloe,
Series Editors

The Dramatic Arts and Cultural Studies
Acting against the Grain

Kathleen S. Berry
with an Introduction by Dorothy Heathcote

Falmer Press
a member of the Taylor & Francis Group
New York and London
2000

Published in 2000 by
Falmer Press
A member of the Taylor & Francis Group
29 West 35th Street
New York, NY 10001

10   9   8   7   6   5   4   3   2   1

Library of Congress Cataloging-in-Publication Data

Berry, Kathleen S.
    The dramatic arts and cultural studies : acting against the grain /
    Kathleen S. Berry ; with an introduction by Dorothy Heathcote.
        p.   cm.—(Garland reference library of social science ; v. 861.
    Teaching and thinking ; v. 2)
    Includes bibliographical references and index.
    ISBN 0-8153-0931-7 (hardcover : alk. paper)—ISBN 0-8153-3727-2
    (pbk. : alk. paper)
    1. Drama in education.   2. Culture—Study and teaching.   I. Title.
    II. Garland reference library of social science ; v. 861.   III. Garland
    reference library of social science. Teaching and thinking ; vol. 2

PN3171 .B44 1999
371.39'9—dc21
                                                                99-049314

Printed on acid-free, 250-year-life paper
Manufactured in the United States of America

Dedicated to
Shirley Steinberg
and
my parents
Florence and James V.

Contents

Preface

How do I write a preface about my teacher? What can I say about Kathy Berry that you won't find in her brilliant text? Can I tell you that she is unique? she sparkles? she is drama? she is dramatic? she is the quintessential teacher? I can say all those things, but at the risk of sounding like Lulu singing to *Sir* in 1966, I will try to say something more.

As a thirty-something returning student in Lethbridge, Alberta, I was anxious to get my teaching degree. I had raised four children past Pampers and wanted to reclaim my own life. Knowing that teaching was as natural to me as shopping, I decided to finish my degree in education. The decision was also made easier as education became about the only alternative to someone who had finished three years of university over a decade before—not too many departments were anxious to take me. So, I became a teacher education student. Again by the process of elimination, since I had never taken high school math or finished my sciences, I chose English/Language Arts as my major.

The first semester was forgettable as a series of modulated mini-classes were thrust down our throats—we learned assessment (how to make up multiple-choice tests), reading diagnostics (how to administer cloze testing), and behavior management (how to modify kids by locking the door to prevent tardies from entering). By the second semester, I was immersed in the skill of teachering. By the fifth class, I was able to turn in a lesson plan utilizing all of Bloom's taxonomy, with barely any corrections—I was on my way to becoming a schoolteacher. Most of my worries lay in the fact that I couldn't quite get grade weighting down to perfection and that my chalkboard writing wasn't dark enough, nor did it adhere to the strict lettering standards expected at most schools of excellence.

I'm sure you are anticipating what my next paragraph will contain. I can't disappoint you. So, without overdramatizing the event, I will just say that I began my second semester with a methods class taught by a new teacher, Berry. She assured us she wasn't a Dr. yet, and we had to call her Kathy. She was quite funky by western Canadian standards—she wore lots of plaids, sweaters, and great necklaces. She acted as if she liked being there, and she quickly assured us she was different from any other professor. Naturally, I was psyched. However, my excitement was quickly crushed when she announced that the entire semester was to be devoted to a subject that historically had established our town, Lethbridge—coal mining.

Other than my sexual/intellectual fascination with D.H. Lawrence and *Sons and Lovers,* I was not a coal mining devotee. The thought of an entire semester devoted to coal mining sounded like a drag. Besides, how could we learn to weight grades, create balanced tests, read standard deviations—basically, how could we become good teachers—if everything were smashed into some silly theme like mining? Not only was Berry going to *make* us learn to teach coal mining, she was not going to delineate which lesson went into which unit. She insisted on teaching something she called *across the curriculum* and cited little known people like David Booth and Shirley Bryce what's-her-name. She told us she had worked and studied with Dorothy Heathcote and assured us that this Dorothy woman knew how to teach. Right.

You can imagine the groans and complaints. I was not happy to spend an entire semester mucking around in the dirty history of Lethbridge's contribution to black lung and explosions. Besides being boring, that was boy stuff and I wasn't interested.

I can't capture on paper exactly what happened to us that semester but we became coal miners. And we became teachers. Using Heathcote's "Teacher in Role" concepts and stretching them into the nether regions of funkiness, Berry had us on the ground with eighty-year-old miners learning to put our boots on, with Rose, a widow who had lost her husband in the explosion in the thirties, and creating volumes of stuff on—well, just on teaching. We researched our butts ("bums" for Canadians) off, we read, we interviewed, we improvised, we acted, we wrote, we performed, and we learned how to be teachers.

Kathy Berry is my mentor. She brought out the teacher in me. I never did learn to weight grades or to understand what the hell a T-score was. But I learned how to teach. I learned to weave theatre and drama throughout every part of my teaching life. I learned to improvise in school and in the world. Kathy Berry taught me to teach, and I thank her.

Shirley R. Steinberg
Adelphi University
New York
November 1999

Acknowledgments

Friends and family are always the foundation to any endeavor. My thanks to Jan Blakey for telling me I'm having fun and that I have a professional sense of humor. Like a bevy of enablers, Mary Lou Stirling was exceptionally considerate and helpful in many aspects of my academic, professional, and personal life. Bill and Barb Laws started it all. To family; Mom, Dad, Bob, Pam, Chris, Mike, Jim, John, Lesley, Auntie Willena and Uncle Paul—the Berrys—you can visit me anytime but I'll still have books in my hands. To Derek and Edwina, "ewe" are generous in dialogue, hospitality, and artistic thought. Wishes came true when David Dillon was my advisor—and for his encouragement I am grateful. I would be amiss if I failed to mention the work of my mentor, Dorothy Heathcote, and her incredible influence on drama. She is a postmodern, poststructuralist, and postcolonial thinker. Her work is deconstruction in action. I am constantly amazed at how her thoughts seem so simple but when in action they push beyond the borders of the modern imagination and create "rhapsodic intellect." Raymond Heathcote graciously tolerates Dorothy's international students, me included, who arrive at the door for tutoring sessions. Without my typists, Allison Duffy, Kerry Casey, Chris Barnes, Brenda Cummings, and Beverlee Stewart, ideas and words would just be misdemeanors imprisoned in my head. Joe Kincheloe, Ian, Megan, Chaim, and the postmodern Bronwyn are important to Shirley—so it follows they are important people somewhere in this book. To my students in Cultural Studies through Theater Classes, I appreciate your patience, as we struggled together through new ideas and practices. I thank Ann Cameron and the students of Lady Beaverbrook

Residence for the addition of dignity and sophistication in my life. Special honor goes to former students like Shirley Steinberg—to whom this book is dedicated—and Debbie Letourneau. To them goes the award for courage to try any of this! Shirley, along with Joe Kincheloe, thank the goddesses, did. She has nurtured, encouraged, and supported me constantly, patiently waiting to edit the next draft, the next page, the next apology—and now this part of the scripting is done. Let the play begin! Any errors or omissions in this book are unintentional and I welcome information in that regard.

Introduction

Dear Kathy,

You asked me to read your treatise (I feel "book" is a bit of an understatement for the detailed warp and weft of your fabric-action!) as if I were an undergraduate interested in a possible relationship between contemporary theories of cultural studies, deconstruction of texts, and dramatic arts used in the interests of learning. Well, I just did, and I think you should write in a health warning to support those readers who might decide to incorporate your suggestions into their drama work within the cultural constructions we call schools with all their built-in hegemony. You see how persuasive your specialist language is—it's already affecting mine!

Those brave enough to tackle the notions embedded in your text will need not only to risk applying it in praxis (action in contemplation), learning as they go and picking themselves up when they get out of their depth; they'll also have to face the barbs of the therapists, the soothers, the art-of-the-theatre merchants, and the "let's have f-u-u-u-u-n" advocates. It's a brave soul who deconstructs social encounters, for "nasty things come out of the woodshed."

You make it all sound so exciting, so innocent (but not naïve), that I warm and positively glow in response . . . even to all those quotations you've had to use to prove to academia that you've read the field. Hegemony.

The health warning is your responsibility. Now I shall address your envisaged audience of readers.

Dear Student/Reader,

Now and again you come across academic writing that has a passionate dimension and, when you do, treasure it even when it makes you feel (as I have felt when reading Dr. Berry's work) as if you've been put through rollers, so that all the fixed, organized, safe assumptions are battered, pressurized, hashed up, and rejumbled and you don't know if you're coming or going. Kathy Berry's notion of a symbiotic relationship between dramatic arts and contemporary theories of cultural studies seems to me to present education with a possible new paradigm, and future use-full-ness for the area of learning I've attended to for fifty years—drama *as* education. (Yes, I sound like Methuselah, but I started teaching in university when very young.)

In early September 1996, I learned of a school project that made me wonder if drama as education has reached its sell-by date. Contemplate the situation: Six classes of primary-age children from inner-city schools in Chile, Spain, London (England), Italy, and Africa have all been given computers with the necessary equipment to e-mail one another and use the Internet to share their cultural experiences and interrogate them. The children in the Chile school live on a town dump and can go to school when they've done their stint of scavenging for food. Their first question to their contemporaries in all the other sharing schools—"How do you get bullets out of people in your country?"—certainly made *me* consider whether drama explorations, with the necessary slower exposition, might now be superseded!

I comforted myself in my article about the project with the lame (or so it seemed to me then) proposal that "small groups of children and their leader/teacher are still essential to preserve the stance of interrogating human events through the immediacy of dramatic time and role responsibility." I've been using *stewardship* as my paradigmatic educational stance. Then, serendipitously, the postman dropped through my mail slot Dr. Berry's eloquent and convincingly developed ideas—and a richer paradigm.

She is in good company. Toffler (*The Third Wave*) and Lessing (in her *Skikasta–Canopus in Argos* Archives) both subscribe to Dr. Berry's notion that informed, analytical, culturally sophisticated, and interrogatory-minded children can and should be assumed to be responsible and fully able to share in the development of the affairs of humankind.

Now, readers, you don't have to start at the beginning of her densely packed text (Dr. Berry won't mind—she suggested cheekily that I might use it to prop up the "being-one day" repaired axle of our 1931 car!). Take this image to yourself: that of weaving. All woven fabrics have warp threads, which are long and move from behind (a history) toward a future (that which will become). Fabrics also have weft threads, which run from side to side and create the woven pattern via the action of being trailed through the warp threads, selectively picking them up. Dr. Berry's warp threads are those carefully defined aspects of culture, power, hegemony that we inherit from *our* past and influence in *our* present, thereby endowing *our* descendents with "culture." She develops these later, in Chapters 4 and 5. Her weft threads are the kinds of treatments she evidences and the suggestions placed in Chapter 6—the action chapter. The weft that weaves forms the perceptions we begin to notice as we actively engage with carefully selected warp aspects of culture as it currently and historically exists.

And study most carefully her exposition of the kinds of texts and sites—excellent words for such as I/me, who has only a home-made vocabulary as yet. But who knows what jargon will leave my lips now that I have been introduced to Dr. Berry's nonjargon usage of a particularized discipline?

When you've sorted out the warp and the weft of the ideas in this book, then you'll probably (if you expect to live long!) want to study the ore that Dr. Berry has patiently mined and signposted for you in the earlier chapters—as academics properly should. You shouldn't have to reinvent her wheel, so make use of it.

As Dr. Berry has spent quite a lot of time on the historical aspects of cultural studies, may I offer you, the reader, an event I saw recently in an English infant school. Young children were interrogating a cultural aspect of English royalty. The position they queried was related to that of "one queen at a time" in England. Henry VIII, as you probably know, married six ladies at different times. The problems he faced throughout his reign (apart from needing to beget an heir—male, if possible) was how to dispose of each wife/queen as his eye lit upon a possible successor. The six-year-old children thought that each lady would contribute different qualities to our culture and concluded it was a waste to cut off their heads or seclude them in convents "to be good." They provided a solution (remember, being only six, they do like tidy endings! Dr. Berry, being somewhat older, prefers more open outcomes!), and it seems eminently suitable for contemplation by such as you and me—and Dr. Berry. They advised Henry (in the shape of Dr. Johntines, an eminent history scholar) to "call them all Catherine"—that being the name of queen/spouse number one—"and bring out the most suitable one for any cultural occasion." I'm currently pondering . . . deconstructing . . .

Dorothy Heathcote

THE DRAMATIC ARTS
AND CULTURAL STUDIES

CHAPTER 1

A Modern World in Crisis

PROMPTING THE READER

Dorothy Heathcote (Wagner, 1976), the leading drama educator, once stated: "Drama is about humans in a mess." One of the first premises of this book is that the world is in a mess, or crisis—a crisis of knowledge, values, behavior, events, institutions, text, representations, images, film, history, and of political, social, and economic structures. In fact, any aspect of modern life is subject to interrogation or scrutiny through the dramatic arts. How convenient for participants and spectators—from directors to playwrights, actors, stage managers, costume designers, drama educators and students, and many others, including audiences. Informed by contemporary theories, modern life is undergoing a transformation of content, form, and structure, as are many of the arts, sciences, and other disciplines. The purpose of this book is to make accessible to undergraduates, graduates, and others in education, theater, and drama, the theories and practices of contemporary philosophical stances borrowed from deconstructionism, critical theory, cultural studies and criticism, postmodernism, poststructuralism, and postcolonialism. Although the boundaries of knowledge between these areas are blurred and many times cross over, the distinction between disciplines, between conceptualizations, between content and form, is clouded by the very knowledge that informs these contemporary theories and practices.

When we locate ourselves in the theories of cultural studies and criticism—that is, the position from where we are sitting, standing, living, thinking, or teaching; raising a family; practicing in churches, universities, business, or other institutions—radical philosophical changes happen. Thus the implications of contemporary theories and practices for the dramatic arts, especially in pedagogical contexts, are lavish.

First of all, the field of dramatic arts is multidimensional. To name a few: skits, vaudeville, improvisation, theater, musicals, collective theater, routines, drama, docudrama, process-orientated drama, political theater, dance, carnival, buskers, puppets, mime, cultural theater, story theater, drama across the curriculum, mystery plays, comedy theater, feminist theater, theater of the queer, classical theater, Asian theater such as Kabuki, children's theater, children's film, children's animation, and children's live theater, television, video, multimedia, performance art, chamber theater, readers' theater, circus, scripted theater, creative dramatics, agit prop, choral reading, opera, promenade, community theater, pantomime, burlesque, reviews, spectacles, ceremony, pageants, rituals, street theater, and a host of other forms.

To a cultural critic, each of these dramatic art forms is available for scrutiny and interrogation by contemporary cultural theories and practices. In no way does this suggest that the dramatic arts will be any more creative in the future. They have always moved forward through the avant garde but, at times, have also reached static points. However, what happened in the past is happening in the present, and it will challenge the roots, content, and structures of any of the arts and, in many cases, create new ways of thinking and reflecting on the world. Possibilities of re-vising, re-visiting, re-writing, re-staging, re-constructing, and re-thinking the world is the contribution of cultural studies and criticism. The dramatic arts follow suit.

The major functions of these contemporary theories and practices are to interrogate, investigate, disrupt, and intervene in the cultural constructions of modern life in order to disrupt content, structures, and images that marginalize or oppress; that flaunt power; that are ethnic cleansing, abusive, invisible; that are unnecessarily desirable and seductive; that privilege or value one knowledge paradigm over another; that silence or stereotype; that are rigidly authoritative; that background a particular gender, race, class, or physicality, intelligence, or sexuality that is different from that of the dominant or mainstream. The discourse of contemporary theories talks about inclusions, fringes, control, domination, oppression, disengagement, restrictions, and the forgotten.

In what do contemporary theories and practices intervene? They interrogate the status quo generally, that is, the dominant epistemology (knowledge and ways of knowing), the dominant ontology (being and

way of being), the ways of industry, symbols, values, behavior, proce-
dures, methods, policies, disciplines, experiences, beliefs, relationships,
truths, structures, ideas, institutions, rituals, and a host of many other
constructions of modern society, including texts of any symbolic representation, technologies of modern media (such as radio, television, film,
computers), and the context of our daily lives. Every construction, in its
turn and at the same time, is available for interrogation and interruption
by contemporary theories and practices, especially within the flexibility
of a dramatic arts' rehearsal process.

Questions of cultural studies and criticism intervene and interrogate
the domination and devaluing of all realms of existence based on differences within and between gender, race, class, sexuality; nationality,
ethnicity, religion, and history; of local, geographical, and regional differences; of linguistic, physical, and mental differences; and a host of
other possible cultural constructions. Situated within cultural criticism,
any dramatic arts' performance challenges and questions the genocen-
tric, phallocentric, logocentric, ethnocentric, and Eurocentric world of
culture and acts as a challenge to the homologue of modern science and
technology; objective, Euro-American male rationality; reductionism,
essentialism, biologism, naturalism, technologism, and Cartesian dualism upon which modern society is constructed.

This conceptual, rather esoteric, terminology will be discussed and,
hopefully, evolve into a clearer understanding for practitioners in the dramatic arts. Theories and practices performed through the dramatic arts
demand challenges to constructions, marginalizations, concepts, differences, and the centrisms of contemporary society. The attitude asserted
by these theories encourages disruptions, interruptions, interrogation, investigations, interventions, interdisciplinary and cross-disciplinary blurring, plurality, and interchangeable portrayals of realities. Divergence,
diversity, dismantling, and decentering of dominant, fixed, controlling,
and legitimized powers are central to the responsibilities of cultural critics. In addition, a key concept of cultural criticism, as a theory of political action, includes hegemony, a term used to frame the process of
cultural construction that remains unchallenged and thus maintained and
circulated by consent. As dramatic artists engaged in cultural criticism,
interrogations and dismantling of modern life begets, we intellectually
assume, counter-hegemony.

Each of these areas of modernity are considered sites, contexts,
texts, textuality, worlds, or positions from which we speak, think, perform, interrogate, and challenge. To do so, think of the prefix "re," which

means "again," not necessarily as a direction for looking at totally new visions, new ideas, or new knowledge, but as a re-thinking, re-rooting, re-visiting, re-hearsing, re-enactment, re-claiming, re-authoring, and re-covery of the content and structures of modern life in order to dismantle them. Cultural critics engage in re-imagining, re-flexivity, re-flecting, re-sisting, re-inserting, re-presenting, re-inventing, re-acting, re-membering or re-memory, re-enchanting, re-constructing, re-verberating, re-mapping, re-generating, re-charting, re-grounding, re-informing, re-positioning, re-cognizing, re-conditioning, and re-structuring. From these sites, we re-think and re-write our autobiographies, biographies, voices, subjectiv-ities, positions, history, knowledge, values, structures, and institutions. The world, as culturally constructed, is made available to the scrutiny of cultural criticism. In the end, life is re-positioned, and margins are moved to the center to be shared equally.

This brainstorming introduction is not intended to sound evangelical, but to rehearse or provide a prompt for the application of contemporary theories. Some rather esoteric terminology is discussed, such as decon-structionism, posthumanism, postcolonialism, postmodernism, and post-structuralism; multiple realities, multiple endings, multiple beginnings, multiple interruptions, multiple views, multiple resistances, multiple di-mensions, multiple possibilities; anti-psychologisms, serendipity, contin-gency, flux, counter-memory, disengaging; an archaeology of life. Thus, it is the peeling back of the layers of culture to see and rethink the world in new ways. It requires a willingness to participate in counter-memory, and counter-hegemonic theories and practices that allow us to intervene in all of these constructions of modern society and move us into postmodern constructions. We have replacements or repositioning of status, for exam-ple, cross-cultural, cross memories, mixed genres, mixed marriages, dis-placements; making the familiar strange; border crossing; blurring the boundaries between knowledge, values, truths, and ideas; blurring the un-differentiated boundaries between concepts, worlds, ideas; the nomadic kind of movement where we are, at one point, homeless, living in the flux of contemporary theories and practices, yet positioned in the world by gender, race, class, age, history, and other symbolic artifacts that shape who we are and how we think and how we say and do.

A major source that structures and controls consciousness and polit-ical action in modern life is discourse that creates and frames culture. Modern discourses have locked us into conceptual formations, govern and limit our lives and imaginations, prejudge how we are to live in fam-ilies and public institutions. Grand narratives or grand theories and their discourses, created by modern society, dominate how we think and act socially, personally, and intellectually.

Theories and practices of cultural studies and criticism demand that we unpack the contradictions and restrictions of our modern world including the historical, traditional, and mythological. Cultural critics contemplate paradigms that govern and direct our lives generally and specifically, including the content and structures of the dramatic arts. We wonder when and how articulations of the private that move into public realms reveal worlds that remain politically dangerous to speak about in a world of "grand narratives" and dominant, modern institutions such as church, school, family, community, big business, or government. We hear constantly, through the power of modern technology, the discourses perpetuated by institutions that structure our consciousness in ways that silence differences and resistances or evoke consent. Our world becomes very apolitical and hegemonic with no space, desire, or guts for resistance or political action. We look at the sins of the past, of imperialism and colonialism, the dominance of the Empire in which whole populations and their cultural values and knowledge were abolished.

The imposition and intervention of modern technologies, for example, television, film, and computers, produce hyper-realities where the textures of the human and the textures of technology blur the boundaries between what is real and what we think is real, in which what is constructed in hyper-realities and technologies is as real as everyday life. As Baudrillard (1988) calls it, "the simulacra."

Finally, it means keeping our sense of humor. If nothing else, the dramatic arts allows us to explore, to play, to be ludic (playful), to dance with all of these perspectives. We can use humor, irony, parody, analogy, comedy, and intellectual sarcasm. We can meander with metaphors or travel with tropes (figures of speech); we move without, nor aim for, closure to ideas, challenges, history, knowledge, or values. As the song goes, "everything old is new again." This is the burden, both as academics, as students, as pedagogues, as layperson, and as dramatic artists. So what is so fun and what are the promises?

At best, like most promises, they are contingent upon a certain solidarity about all this—not as conformity or consensus, but as solidarity. Modern life is in crisis. The dramatic arts are in crisis, as is the construction of subjectivity and identity, and institutional structures that control and sustain modernity. These crises require a solidarity that does not guarantee us, but allows us to move back and forth between the crisis, promises, hopes of emancipation and freedom, justice and change,

transformations and fulfillment of desires, liberation, alterity, and celebration. Needless to say, these are extremely big promises.

We are eyewitnesses. We are testimonies to modern culture. We have
confessions. We have sinned as have our fore-parents. The dramatic arts
grants us the promise of exploration and playfulness, with possibilities,
with a sense of seriousness, and also with a ludic temperament. Contemporary theories encourage the ludicrous. Through the agency of the dramatic arts informed by cultural studies and criticism, we can consider the
crisis of modern life and rehearse possible re-imaginings.

The previous textual excursions were not intended as an intellectual
pep rally, but as a way of leading the naive and curious reader into further
investigations through cultural studies and criticism, with added implications for the dramatic arts and pedagogy.

INTRODUCTION TO TERMINOLOGY

In order to proceed with a degree of clarity, I would like to introduce some
of the major terminology of this book. One of the key words is "world."
We talk about the world as socially constructed. In other words, what exists in the world did not come into existence on its own. Cultural constructions such as institutions and language, and the formations of our selves,
knowledge, and truths are all social constructions. A world is not a geographical globe, but includes the world of knowledge, truths, languages,
discourses, subject disciplines, history, and symbolic representations.

Another term considers the world as text. Traditionally, text meant
anything that is print. The world, in cultural studies and criticism, means
any symbolic representation that contains shared symbols, meanings,
representations, rituals, knowledge, or other elements. A text can be visual, printed, oral, theoretical, or practical. Context means the historical,
social, political, intellectual, or economic location in which the text has
been created or constructed.

"Reality" is another word that tends to appear quite frequently in the
literature. Reality is constructed by human thoughts and discourse, not as
something that exists naturally or outside human symbolic ordering of
the world. Perceptions and points of view depend upon where we are located in history, space, geography, gender, race, and class, and they are
accorded a positioning, so to speak. We have multiple realities; so standing from my position as a white, middle-class, middle-aged, Canadian,
academic woman, reality is perceived, challenged, written, and constructed in a particular way.

WHAT IS IN CRISIS?

At this point, I will begin the discussion about worlds, texts, contexts, and realities in crisis. According to contemporary theories, aspects and constructions of modern life and human endeavors are in crisis. It does not mean they have disappeared; it does not mean that we have criticized them; it is not about the dualism of positive and negative. The world is "in a mess." Modern constructions are problematic because they exclude in texts, contexts, and worlds. Certain knowledge, truths, race, age, sexuality, subjectivity, authorship, borders, values, histories, and a host of other cultural constructions are all problematic. We are positioned, and how we are positioned adds to the difficulty of entering the world, revisioning it as inclusive of all knowledge, truths, subjectivities, and other earlier-mentioned constructions.

Important to the study of cultural formations is the primacy of the political. In other words, the world is conflict-ridden in which the primacy of the political makes the world and its texts contested landscapes full of struggle, disasters, and despair. The burden of cultural studies and criticism is to challenge and question the terrain, not necessarily to solve the crisis or problems, but at least to acknowledge and recognize the conditions and begin to act politically—that is, to gain power to change. Auslander (1992) claims that "the notion of choice that calls for important discriminations and decisions is in crisis" (p. 2). The purpose of this text is to articulate, rehearse, and reveal possibilities, and to examine crisis in order that important choices, discriminations, and decisions can be made. In this particular case, I am interested in attaching cultural studies and criticism to the dramatic arts.

Another important factor that we must accept is the notion that the world is in crisis, brought about by, and framed by, modern life. Modern life has perpetuated major crises such as modern warfare, nuclear threat, severe ecological crisis, Auschwitz, the Gulag, disarmament, economic exploitation of devalued and colonized populations, large monopolies in business and government, and rising terrorism and daily violence. In fact, every aspect of modern life in some way or other is in crisis.

A variety of terminology to describe modern life includes "modernization," "modernity," and "modernism." Each of these categories affords us a categorical framework with which to work. The debate flourishes among the theoreticians, philosophers, historians, and others as to what marks the beginning point of the modern age and if, indeed, it is ended or is beginning to end, *fin de siècle*. Whatever point is chosen will not become a major issue here. Adam and Tiffin (1990) claim that modernism belongs to the notion of cultural practices, modernization is the economic process with social and cultural implications, and modernity is the philosophical category designating the temporality of the post-traditional world. Auslander (1992) states that modernity and modernism "have created an individual who cannot understand the causes of crisis and therefore cannot make political decisions" (p. 21). The intent of this book is to provide some theoretical articulations and interventions in modern life through the rehearsal process of the dramatic arts as a forum that illuminates crises in modern life and energizes the political imagination—that is, which activates a ludic postmodernism.

POSITIVISTIC KNOWLEDGE IN CRISIS

One of the major theorists, Descartes, and his theory of positivism seems to be, in many experts' minds, the point at which ontological and epistemological existence broke from traditional life and moved the world toward modern life. The philosophy of Descartes, known as Cartesianism, separates the world as subjective and objective. Prior to this point, knowledge, truth, life was holistic. If we are truly engaged in a dramatic art, even as audience, then body, spirit, mind, knowledge, beliefs, values, and attitudes unite together as one through the dramatic action. However, for our purposes, of course, these constructions of mind, body, and spirit are socially, culturally, and historically conditioned, and, therefore, influence how we do drama, how we look at modern life, and how we engage the political imagination.

Cartesianism and other underpinnings that emerged from this philosophy have dominated Western modern life. This tradition imposes homogeneity upon the material identity of things and conceptual thought and culminates in the technical triumph of Western rationality, which can know things only in that it comes to dominate them. "Enlightenment relates to things as the dictator to humans" (Benhabib, 1992, p. 208).

Thus begins the initial control, objectification, and rationalization of our world. In other words, knowledge can be controlled and, in turn, can control. Knowledge of our world can be separated out from the knower. This control also invites dominance of knowledge, truths, and other cultural constructions. Again, this is a crisis. If the world is constructed accordingly, we inherit a world of epistemological dualism that imposes universal truths and, in turn, makes the whole notion of truth in crisis.

ABSOLUTE TRUTH IN CRISIS

"That's right," our parents always said, "tell the truth." As children, we knew that what was truth for them and what was truth for us sometimes was problematic, contested, or seen as telling a lie. Truth, in modern life, has been constructed as have other elements of life and seems to exist in some absolute manner—the absolute truth. Thus, it is the knower or social contexts that construct truths. As Auslander (1992) states: "Truth is . . . a convention" (p. 93); people accept and conform to a certain truth and, through time and discourse, preserve it as legitimate and absolute (a hegemonic state).

Indeed, if we accept as "fact" that truth is a convention, then who determines whose and what truth is an issue or crisis when truth is formulated by dominant groups based on the power given to them through the authority and practices of institutions or structures, especially academic truth (typically known as truth that is removed from the real world, or the abstract truth of intellectuals). In addition, truth becomes constructed by dominant groups, and it pressures others not of that group into positions of powerlessness, falsehoods, conformity, and consent (again, subject to hegemonic practices). If truth is determined by a particular group, it becomes exclusive of all other truths, those historical, political, social, local, or international. A statement of truth "denies its own historical construction and ideological perceptions" (Benhabib, 1992, p. 4). Ultimately, it becomes a cultural convention left unchallenged (hegemony).

What constitutes truth? Who attains it? For what purposes? Who does it exclude? Truth in the hands of the powerful excludes other truths. Truth, as constructed and dominant in Western society, has been determined by the enlightenment project that privileges scientific, male, European, white truth. Therefore, based on gender, race, and other factors, most of us are eliminated from the dominating truth of Western society. In fact, with the increasing modernization of Eastern cultures and societies, Asian and African populations are excluded from the dominant frameworks of modern life. We can see this in Asian countries' rush to modernize, to become more Western, not only in production and capital, but in statements of truth.

Truth contained within modern constructs by dominant groups are not necessarily universal, total, or rational, but become the grounds for doubt, questioning, and political decision making. Perhaps for the audience, who might be male, European, white, and so forth, the content and experiences might be true. However, think of the number of spectators and participants in the dramatic arts that are excluded, not just in terms of presence, but knowledge, values, history, and so forth. With each presentation of truth through the dramatic arts, interrogation includes: Whose truth? What truth? Whose interests are these truths serving? When were they constructed, by whom, at what time, and in what space?

These questions challenge the legitimizing process of what constitutes truth in terms of content, process, and presentation for each and all of the dramatic arts—from camp skits to dramatic scripts, from theater as entertainment to theater as political action, to opera and musical. The privilege given to the absolute truths of positivism and science in modern life has become a question of "accessibility and circulation of knowledge by different minds" (McHale, 1989, p. 9). With the dominant group's advantaged position, they define what truth is and contain it within some kind of paradigmatic frame of knowledge. They diminish the world, text, context, and realities to modes of theory and reductive thinking that violates the expansiveness of the dramatic and speculative imagination—the released imagination.

The birth of positivistic science and the human sciences that have legitimized particular knowledge, foregrounded certain truths, and eliminated or devalued other truths and knowledge have managed to sustain "a state managed knowledge, and a manipulation of consciousness and desire" (Agger, 1991, p. 91). Part of this process of schooling, a process of manipulation of use in consciousness, is managed by the state (at one time, the church) in such a way that curriculum theory, development, implementation, and evaluation have decided which curriculum, which knowledge, in what order it will be presented, at what level, and to whom, and in what particular ways. A powerful ideological dominance kept alive by the credibility and legitimizing means given to state-managed knowledge of government-induced curriculums and districts, and consented to by public consumers, is hegemony in action.

Several teachers do address issues that contain particular knowledge about the world, people, relationships, situations, or historical events that need to be challenged; that is, they not only teach what is legitimatized by the dominant paradigms of science, but the truths that are needed for the reproduction of existing social arrangements. With this in mind, the dramatic arts are a means for scrutiny and interrogation of the crisis of truth. Theories and practices in the dramatic arts move into another realm—the realm of cultural studies and other contemporary theories (to be discussed in Chapter 2).

Privileging state-managed knowledge determines the social and political formations of our consciousness. Most readers of this text probably are situated within a classroom context—within the space and time allocations of state-managed knowledge and manipulations, with a timetable that not only determines the time in which to gather, interpret, understand, and evaluate the knowledge, but also within calculated units that create disciplinary boundaries such as the dramatic arts, science, history, language arts, social studies, health, and so forth.

The message sent by Cartesian dualism and positivism reaches into daily life and determines how we construct and are constructed by modern life. Dramatic arts fall into this disciplinary construct. Without the recognition that knowledge, disciplines, and truths are constructed by dominant groups that exclude others, based on difference from the mainstream group, power circulates and maintains "the politics of instrumental rationality generated by the logic of capital "(Adam and Tiffin, 1990, p. 140). Students involved in disciplinary areas are no longer educated but are products and objects of capital. In other words, the amount and kind of learning becomes valid and legitimate, an epistemological capital (capital of knowledge) so to speak, that is salable in the job marketplace.

Participants in the dramatic arts know very well that the value given to the knowledge and truths gained during the rehearsal process and performance are not privileged. In my experience, most curricula across North America do not include the dramatic arts. If they do so, it is very specific in what part they play. Then, of course, many students take dramatic arts in high school and university because it is an "easy" course. Traditional norms of what really constitutes rigorous learning and thinking is left to the sciences and technology.

MODERN INSTITUTIONS IN CRISIS

One of the major outcomes of modernity/ism/ization, has been the creation of bureaucratic institutions, that is, divisions of control. Institutions often enable

> things to function, inaugurate new modes of knowledge, initiate productive associations, offer assistance and support, provide useful information, create helpful social ties, simplify large scale problems, protect the vulnerable and enrich the community. Typically, institutions explain events, normalize behavior, regulate values, prompt efficiency, package information, organize interests, centralize authority,

> hierarchies, and constituents, erect borders, prescribe pleasure, license
> play, institute discipline, banish deviance, maintain the status quo, en-
> gage in self promotion, rationalize particular interests, bureaucratize
> thought and activity, solicit obedience, mechanize bodies and gender
> opposition. Without institutions there is no community. (Leitch, 1992,
> p. 128)

The dynamics of institutions frequently tend toward abuse, exclusion, marginalization, and devaluing of nondominant cultural constructions, whether knowledge, truth, class, race, gender, and so forth. The authority given to modern institutions, ranging from family to schools, from church to military, and from government to big business has created edifices of authority to claims of truth, knowledge, theories, and expertise.

The organization and centralization of powerful political, economic, and social systems determines knowledge as capital. Institutions regulate and control truth, knowledge, disciplines, and theories. Academic institutions, the context in which this book is written, control truth and knowledge as capital (publish or perish), and compartmentalize knowledge and truth through disciplines such as science, engineering, mathematics, natural sciences, human sciences, professional schools, social studies, second language learning, music, art and—yes—the dramatic arts (dominated by the theatrical performance attitude of "why haven't you put on a play?"). Those of us learning, working, reading, and living within institutional constructions are also shaped by their power, shaped in imagination, word, and deed. Daily life is conducted in the institution and keeps us within the constraints of modernity. Modern institutions as privileged centers, not of crisis in and of themselves, but as a crisis of modernity, are problematic in a postmodern world. Bureaucratic programs, workshops, and courses that provide crisis intervention and management strategies address only the "surface aspects of social and political problems and constantly defer grappling with real causes" (Auslander, 1992, p. 21).

Although we cannot imagine modern society without institutions, from the personal to the public ones, they have severe implications for study of the world and text, especially through the dramatic arts. In addition, with so much knowledge received by teachers and students through narrative forms such as television programming, learning shows or situation comedies, sports channels and video story programs, media institutions are another source of the imposition of modernity on the constructions of truth, knowledge, and subject disciplines.

MODERN VALUES AND ETHICS IN CRISIS

The institutionalization of truth, knowledge, and disciplines places modern values and ethics in crisis. Modernity has totalized not only the claims to reason, but has argued for a social ethics based upon itself without moral or philosophical grounds. As Rorty (1989) argues, modern life has become more interested in knowledge as fact than in knowledge as how to act morally and ethically. There is no need to reiterate that the dominance of modern values—in particular, values based on a dominant gender, race, class, sexuality, physical and mental abilities, and a host of other categories of different cultural constructions—is in a state of crisis.

In the late twentieth century, as capitalism dominates both Western and Eastern culture, claims made by capitalist proponents, for example, about social support systems, say that it is not a crisis of modernity but a crisis of socialism. In the acceptance of dominant Western capitalist values, all aspects of life are a commodity to be bought, sold, and traded like stocks and bonds on Wall Street.

"The obvious point is that values themselves operate within and across a complex and dense network of accepted and contested notions, categories, beliefs, conventions, images and codes" (Leitch, 1992, p. 1). We are not only totalizing rationality, truth, knowledge, and epistemology, but also our ontological value system—our way of being and living. What we value are the capitalistic, commodified features of our lives. In the dramatic arts, the dominance of the glitz of Hollywood or the big musical productions of an Andrew Lloyd Webber play pay homage and condescend to particular values. The surface becomes more important—the shine and the materialism. In turn, bourgeois culture and capital determine what and how we value.

HISTORICAL IMAGINATION IN CRISIS

Years ago, I was interviewing an eighty-seven-year-old woman for a video, and she mentioned her return to university to do a BA in history. She was proud to say she was getting all A+'s. "Of course," she said, "I've been there for most of it" (history). A charming story; however, it is also dangerous if indeed the A+'s are because of an acceptance of what has been taught and left unchallenged. I wonder how much of what she studies truly includes her story, as a Canadian, white, middle-class senior woman with urban roots. The other day, somebody said, "You can't change history, you can't change the facts." My response was, "I hope so and I need to"—we need to. Knowledge of the past is in crisis in modern life. Questions such as: whose history? where am I in that history? how are the stories of race and gender included? excluded? represented within the historical stories? need to be asked. History is used to inform the present and future, but also is abused. Stereotyped, dominant versions of history and forgetting the silenced, the marginalized, and the invisible are a few examples of histories in crisis.

History renders most lives invaluable, devalued, invisible, or silenced. Nietzsche (1957), in his book *On the Advantage and Disadvantage of History for Life,* categorizes history into three areas as follows: monumental history, which is strengthened by vision, where we go on our way more courageously, and we celebrate in national holidays and remembrance days; ancestral history, which gives thanks to existence from the origins, for example, the restoration of ancestral homes and stories to preserve the past; and, finally, critical history, in which people who are oppressed by some present misery want to throw off the burden at all costs, that is, judging and condemning history to shatter and dissolve something to enable him or her to live, keeping parts alive that are challenged by judging, interrogating, and condemning. In a way, these three categories profile an understanding of what and whose stories we use or abuse.

Each category needs to be criticized and/or moved to a state of crisis. Monumental history means to gaze around a neighborhood for statues, monuments, and plaques and ask, Whose history do we celebrate? Most often, it is the wars and battles of white males. When the ancestral story is brought forth we understand our origins. At the same time, personal history has been silenced. For example, abuse of women and children, alcoholism, and other social issues have been relegated or deleted from the history books, as have oral histories of families and communities. Critical history, even in Nietzsche's book, was written from a European male's point of view. The author does not challenge his own critical history; nor does his translated text of 1980, which is in male-gendered language. Whether it is monumental, ancestral, or even critical history, where do differences based on gender, race, class, physicalness, mental absolutes, or history play a role?

Sometimes there is a deliberate elimination or distortion of the historical facts. Where are the stories of women? Where were they during the past? Were they relegated totally to the household chores? Were they hunting and yet devalued because men were the cooks?

As a maritimer, on the east coast of Canada, I have a history that eliminates the role of women in Canadian history. Even deeper and more problematic, and in crisis, is that the history of eastern Canada and of North America should be in the hands of Native Americans. If they were to tell their story, history books would contain different perspectives on the past, and different notions of knowledge, values, politics, gender, and so forth.

I once sat in a twelfth-grade history class where the student teacher, an excellent storyteller who was well liked by all the students, knew the content of the books he had placed in front of them. I wondered, however, how history was being constructed by and for the women in the class. The constitution of the class was mainly of white, European-descent, middle-class students with a mixture of immigrants from Arab and Asian countries, and also Native Americans. The lesson was about Greek history, which celebrated not only the rise of European modern history and ancient Greek history, but mainly was based on battles. There was a romantic feeling surrounding the lesson. Each student was able to draw maps and recall the facts. No one, however, challenged these facts; no one asked where the women were, no one asked who was oppressed or devalued by Greek history. And, for students, teachers, and parents who claim to want to live in peace, they certainly knew a lot about war stories. The history seems to be focused around war, not about the broader social aspects of humanity. Most people of my generation who were schooled in the 1940s and the 1950s, have no knowledge about, for example, Afro-American and Afro-Canadian history. What knowledge I do have of these histories is told mainly from the master/slave tradition and privileges and honors whites as heroes, even to relating rescue and release stories. In other words, Afro-Canadian and Afro-American people are positioned in history by the dominant white consciousness. African and Asian history are national histories that tend to dominate over personal histories, over gender histories, or over class histories. We still seem to celebrate national histories, whether it is Asian, Greek, Chinese, African, without a knowledge of other kinds of histories.

As Agger (1991) states, public life today is characterized by the loss of memory. Events happen so quickly that memory (solidarity with the dead), like most historical thought, is degraded or misrepresented. Historicity, the experience of the possibilities of social changes, is crucial for liberation. A particular kind of memory, however, is lost. Perhaps it is the memory of the monumental or the ancestral. Maybe history is studied or presented in a manner that never demands application of critical and contemporary theories. Aston (1995) relates how the discovery that her ancestors are female enables her to rethink that the destructive history of the human race is made by men.

Where and when do religious, national, cultural, or state/provincial borders create more problems than effective solutions? Quebec, a province of Canada, talks about separation and becoming a distinct society for the French Canadian population. English culture, money, jobs, and language still dominate French Canadians. They still imagine that their young people in the future will be dominated by the English Canadian world. If history lessons are constructed by the English Canadian imagination, separation and, perhaps, war may be imagined as the only route to achieve distinction for French Canadians. The lesson of history, however, is similar to the balkanization of Europe in which small groups separated and created borders that led to war.

The crisis is that we have not problematized the notions of historical knowledge, which, left unproblematized, leaves future citizens in crisis. History as a curriculum discipline, positivistic in nature, and objective in format and style as constructed by the typical textbook format, dominates our ontological, epistemological, and historical imagination.

What are the sources and consequences of these constructions? asks Toni Morrison (1992). Positioned as an Afro-American woman writer, she re-narrates, re-writes, and represents the history of Afro-American women and America through the literary and academic imagination. She re-positions them historically and presents the struggles and history not as dependent on the power of Occidentals, but as active, strong, political agents against the white imagination. Knowledge, truth, values, curriculum, and dramatic presentations and representations are always historically situated. Recognition of the crisis within the historical imagination, constructed by dominant races, gender, classes, political agendas, and exclusive of or misrepresented by marginal, silenced, or invisible histories is not a call for a death of history. Revisiting, rewriting, and rethinking how we can and do come to have knowledge of the past, to see the past not as an object of knowledge in the present but as a position from which we can act in the future, revitalizes the past to revitalize the future. To do so means to painfully challenge and dismantle modern history and move toward a postmodern historical imagination. Dramatic arts, especially in education, are safe and intellectual sites from which to rehearse those possibilities.

MYTHOLOGY AND TRADITIONS IN CRISIS

A large part of the crisis of truth, knowledge, values, and histories in modern society is the logos—that is, the rational, objectifying, positivistic ordering of our world, text, and context. Another part of our localized and distant world is ordered by the stories of mythology—the mythos. Unlike the rational objectivity of the logos, the mythos organizes our world through the mysterious, mystical, adventurous action and romance of the unfamiliar. Young children live in this world, a world ordered as much by fantasy as by fact, as much by the mythos as by the logos. Each of us at some time or another have been exposed symbolically to our local and distant mythos of other countries, peoples, areas, events, and so forth. Whether old wives' tales or grandparents' tales, whether tall tales, legends, or mystery stories, our truths, knowledge, values, and history are colored by the mythos. Stephen Spielberg, for example, has managed to enchant us with a series of mythologically based films such as *Raiders of the Lost Ark* (1981).

Whether printed, oral, or video text, each rendering of mythology in the context of modernism is in crisis. The content and structures of the mythos are theoretically in crisis in late modernist society. Along gender lines, for example, women know all too well the constraints and limitations of the mythos. Cinderella myths and other "handsome prince" promises have influenced how we constructed reality as young girls and in turn constituted our adult lives ranging from family and other institutional relationships, to both our private and public lives. Further gender issues arise when the heroes are always male—they who act are men. In other words, those to be rescued are female, patiently and passively waiting to be rescued. As Alyssia, a seven-year-old student, asks, "Why are the heroes always boys?"

Tales, legends, and myths told about long-ago cultures, histories, places, groups, and other worldly constructions have either stereotyped, misrepresented, or been distorted over time. A Japanese woman reading folktales to a class of second-grade Canadian students found the stories very disturbing. The woman hoped that the children did not really think that this was the way Japanese are constructed in thought, word, deeds, relationships, and history. She hoped that the young students would see the uncomfortable and untrue position in which these stories placed the Japanese.

Missing from the mythos are the multiple story worlds of different sexualities, physicalities, and mentalities, and a host of other cultural realities and structures. In fact, left unquestioned, we could continue to leave our socially constituted world as constituted by the mythos in crisis without any displacement or moving beyond modern life as constituted by the mythos. Several of the stories, if not all of the stories told through the mythos, are usually told by a dominant, imperial culture that privileges its culture and language over the traditions and stories about whom it is telling the story (Ashcroft, Griffiths, and Tiffin, 1989, p. 26). Within our everyday life, those stories that contain the crisis placed upon modern life through the constructions or the influence of the mythos should be dismantled.

CULTURAL AESTHETICS IN CRISIS

Aesthetics are cultural representations and forms that define love, beauty, truth, justice, and dignity. The arts have traditionally served as a major means of aesthetic expression; mediums that give shape to the shifting historical and cultural definitions of aesthetic life. Like other areas of modern life, however, cultural aesthetics are also in crisis.

Appropriate, at this time, is a discussion of the Walt Disney studio's acquisition of the American Broadcasting Corporation network. Gradually, cultural production is in the hands of a very few, and, in the hands of Hollywood and American film and media, "we are losing the very means of cultural production itself" (Denzin, 1991, p. 71). Certain cultural aesthetics are dominant and accepted through a process of desire, seduction, taken-for-grantedness, and consent (hegemony). Separate from historical processes, reality becomes socially conditioned, especially by mass media. Without a doubt, the dominance of mass, popular culture permeates everyday life, colonizing not just living rooms, but consciousness, where values, knowledge, truths, beauty, and justice are defined by popular mediums as modern aesthetics.

In early modern times, elitist aesthetics dominated; in other words, high culture was only accessed by the very rich and certain classes. Elitism is a type of marginalization that usurps aesthetic power away from the masses. In the late twentieth century, however, with the dominance and easy access of popular culture, there are blurred and mixed categories and genres between elitist and popular aesthetics (Hutcheon, 1988). The opaque distinctions between elitist and mass culture is less aesthetic than the critical distance imposed by a purely high culture. Aesthetics, like art, becomes a commodity for consumption by a mass population and, inserted into this hyper-reality, a take-it-for-granted attitude that popular culture's saturation of our aesthetic world is natural and normal. Masses believe the world is meant to be so, so much so that it dominates cultural logic. Both elementary school and university students with whom I work will include rationales borrowed heavily from popular culture, that is, television, magazines, video, film, music, and the surplus of other cultural technologies that have permeated not only their everyday lives but their logic, notions of truth, justice, love, and beauty. One student quoted the *Seinfeld* show as justification for using certain language in a context that was very demeaning for some members present. Some students are quoting lawyers, doctors, DNA experts, forensic investigators, and a host of other "experts" from the trials of Anita Hill, O.J. Simpson, and Susan Smith. The impact of Oprah Winfrey legitimizes truth, beauty, law, and even political action. My mother, in her uninformed Pollyanna manner, feels Kathy Lee Gifford is a model woman—"more women should be like her" (in spite of Gifford's recent political actions, through media, to stop child labor exploitation).

Traditionally excluded realms of aesthetic expertise were accessible only to a few. The new information technologies, however, have turned aesthetics into a theatrical spectacle that becomes the dominant cultural logic (Denzin, 1991, p. 78). One sixth-grade student was already using the discourse of the O.J. Simpson trial to legitimize his constant bullying of classmates on the playground. But this is not to claim that *Seinfeld,* the Simpson trial, and other mass media popular cultural technologies cause the effects discussed earlier. The concern is about the power and dominance of mass culture especially as cultural capital and logic that eliminates critique of an aesthetics that constitutes our everyday notions and actions regarding truth, beauty, love, and justice. The crisis occurs when mass media and the information industry "connect the ideological with the aesthetic" (Hutcheon, 1988, p. 195) to the degree of establishing cultural cohesion about matters of aesthetics, thus neutralizing reality and leaving the cultural and social totality of our lives left unchallenged. Ultimately, a bourgeois culture is fostered, thereby reinforcing personal, state, and cultural hegemony (a state of uncritical, unchallenged oppression) due to seductive economic, political, and social forces (Auslander, 1992).

The "collective intelligence" (Agger, 1991) dominates aesthetic construction to the impression and marginalization of aesthetic depth and recognition of nonbourgeois realities or worlds. Baudrillard, like Marshall McLuhan, "argues that mass media has neutralized reality for us; first reflecting then masking reality, then masking the absence of reality and finally baring no relation to reality at all" (Hutcheon, 1988, p. 8). Labeled as "simulacrum" by Baudrillard, mass media becomes the site for the final destruction of meaning and truth, and realities cease to be problematic. Implications of cultural aesthetics for the dramatic arts intervene in the modern processes of production. In this world, cultural studies and criticism are involved in the dramatic processes and performance. The entire range of participants from actor to playwrights, from directors to stage managers, from audiences to dramatic educators are obligated to share equally the means of aesthetic production and not succumb to the political and economic pressures of bourgeois, capital gain, or mass media simulacrum, but use it as content to be dramatically dismantled.

Although a distant dream, the dramatic arts' processes and strategies dismantle modern theater, theories, and techniques, and form an attempt to foreground and privilege (both politically and economically) works that critique modern cultural aesthetics, including the dramatic arts itself, and move toward an inclusive kind of aesthetics. Feminist and queer theater have struggled to change the modernized cultural route of exclusion. Since charity begins at home, the first step is for dramatic artists, participants, and spectators to engage cultural critical theories that interrogate, disrupt, and, with no end in mind, resist closure.

REPRESENTATIONS IN CRISIS

The means of cultural representation is another site from which to view the crisis of modern life. Similar to the battle for the control of cultural aesthetics in modern life, the quest for control of artifacts of cultural representation, especially those that represent gender, race, class, physical and mental differences, sexuality, religious, national and ethnic ideologies, and so forth, is jeopardized by modernity. Representations become "regions of signification" (Lash, 1989), to the point of becoming the social and cultural realities, or determining how reality is to be, more so than narrowing reality to the symbolic. In other words, representations are an ideological vehicle for formulating social, political, personal, and institutional significance of this crisis emerging from the impact upon the consciousness. I wonder how a young child or uninformed reader, listener, viewer must view representations of reality. Representations can act as unmediated access to reality and appear to the novitiate as natural and eventually become comfortable conventions of reality. Take-for-granted representations are linked to consciousness as natural phenomenon, like trees, rocks, and wind—some godlike power created them, not humans. When representations control our lives by creating desire, we are led by the neutrality of the representation. Just think of the number of young people thinking they "need" air-pumped running shoes, or relationships and matters of ethics that are represented in image but become actuality.

In the dramatic arts in which I have been involved over the past fifty years, from garage playlets to Rogers and Hammerstein musicals, from school concerts to drama across the curriculum, from street theater to children's puppet plays, in most instances, stereotypes have functioned as the content and the structure of the dramatic event. In rare instances, those familiar representations are raised to the level of ecstasy. The art adds new or changed meanings to the cultural codes. Embedded in these moments of artistic highs, cultural forms of a single dominant meaning are dismantled from stereotypical representations.

A student in one of my theater classes was asked to challenge representations that were dramatically portrayed in a tattoo parlor. After being asked to consider the historical constructions of women, she pondered intensely, nervously laughed, and then said, "It's always been like that" (Aston, 1995). It was difficult to have the student dismantle the context of a representational economy organized by men and realize that, historically, representations have been constructed by humans, in our case, by Euro-Amerocentric white men.

Representations are oppressive when differences are marginalized, devalued, invisible, and more importantly, misrepresented. Tina Nichols (1995), a Native American Maliseet, awakened a group of university students to the oppressive, untruthful, misrepresentation of Native American people in a young person's piece of literature. Although I have, for years, made students aware of the stereotypes of Native Americans in literature (they didn't wear feathers nor did they live in tepees nor do anything but hunt all day and night), Tina, positioned as a Native American, realized I was giving attention only to the surface representations, not the deep semiotic structures of Native Americans that had been relegated to the margins or contaminated by colonization.

One of the major sites for cultural representation, especially in the dramatic arts, is the body. For example, only within the past half-decade has homosexuality been represented in television, mainly through situation comedies and soap operas (irony and parody seem initial ways to open cultural constructions for interrogations). Homosexuality has yet to be represented in advertising, education, ideologies, histories, and popular culture. If so, it is done sometimes to the point of invisibility, sometimes to the point of ridicule, and still against the dominant grain of heterosexuality. Controversial representations, such as art photographer Robert Mapplethorpe's works that display homosexuality, are publicly condemned as pornography. The choice to visit or not visit the show is ignored, and representations of homosexuality are relegated to storage "closets," and political inactivity and publicity that become desire as capital.

DIFFERENCES IN CRISIS

Most of us, at some time or other, have taken standardized tests, dressed like everybody else, followed the crowd, thought along similar lines, done what was asked, required, demanded, or expected of us, or followed suit. Conformity in our actions, thoughts, history, discourse, subjectivity, values, knowledge, and so forth have created a world in "fear of diversity that means marginalization in the name of stability and tradition" (Hutcheon, 1989, p. 16).

The dominance of Western culture has relegated non-European countries and cultures to third-class, "third world" citizenry. The mass homogenization of the world through modern capitalist economy, cultural imperialism, mass media, computer technologies and strategies, including the United Nations, big business institutions, church missionaries, and military organizations has standardized the world—the actual "global education" as compared to the theoretical.

Maurice Chevalier, a French actor and singer of "Thank Heaven for Little Girls," when saying "Vive La Differance," was sexist in his view of girls and women instead of valuing their differences based on other features besides their gender or their body as framed by the male gaze. "Differance," as a challenge to the homogenization of the modern world, values differences based on gender, race, physical and mental abilities, ethnic and national qualities, and other cultural and political formations. Within these categories of differences also exists realms of differences. Since most feminist theory has been constituted by white women, recent feminist theory, for example, has been expanded to include the plurality within itself. In other words, instead of speaking for all women, such as women of color, feminism is pluralized as feminisms to include the polyphony of cultural differences of women. Instead of a singular notion of what constitutes a world, the discourses of many areas, such as feminism, literacies, histories, knowledges, truths, and discourses, are pluralized to reflect the world as a plurality—the politics of differences, not the politics of homogenization.

To create a world of differences is one of the burdens of contemporary life. Antidotes to sameness engage us in the "politics of difference" (Myrsiades and Myrsiades, 1994, p. 34), and in the context of this book, the dramatic arts act as an agency that focuses on issues in a manner that is full of playful rehearsals of difference (not stereotypes) in "an ethically challenging and transformative way" (p. 39). The dramatic arts, conscious of its own standardization of representations, subjectivities, forms, and other cultural artifacts educate participants and spectators to the conformity and homogenization of worldly constructions. As mentioned at the beginning of this chapter, one of the major crises of modern life has been the mass genocides of population by European colonization, Russian gulags, by Westernization through mass technologies, and the Aryan slogans that brought about the slaughter of differences (religious, physical, mental, racial, and local).

Backlash to the politics of difference plays itself out in certain systems of regulatory mechanisms such as media, schools, families, religion, universities, state-regulated governments, national patriotism, big business, and yes, academic writings. Realizations of "standards, of any sort, are not arbitrary or universal" (Kelly, 1993, p. 31). Wiping out differences is unethical, unfair, impossible, and only leads to destruction, war, and death. That is the history we have to explore. In other words, "learn the codes [of gender, race, etc.] and better educate [our] selves to difference" (Dolan, 1993, p. 32). The dramatic arts informed by contemporary critical theories celebrate difference and create a rehearsal hall of cultural and political re-imaging.

TEXTS IN CRISIS

One of the major powers in the construction of modern life, minus the impact of media in the late twentieth century, has been the technology of the printing press, which makes available to the masses texts of literature ranging in content and form from autobiography to classics, from poetry to novels, in national and local stories. "Once you have read one Dickens you have read them all." "I do not remember one literature book during my high school years about or by women except Jane Austen and Charlotte Brontë." "What does Keats, Shelley, or Shakespeare have to do with my life as a woman?" are familiar statements by female university students.

The first statement is from a 1990s university student, the latter two are from a woman in her early fifties and a 1990s high school student, respectively. Each one expresses a crisis of modern life—the dominance and influence of the canons of literature ("great works" by certain authors, including drama texts) that, in a Canadian educational context, has meant, traditionally, British male literature (Shelley, Shakespeare, Keats, Byron, and the rest of the old boys' network) with a smattering of American literature (mostly Mark Twain, William Faulkner, Arthur Miller), and the token Canadian canons of McLennan, Leacock, Carmen, and Sir Charles G. D. Roberts. These works are distributed as sacred texts and hold privileged positions in the curriculum. Although literature was studied for its literary value and as texts that mirror life, limited to nil attention was given to the fact that it also "structures and reproduces" life (Denzin, 1992, p. 138).

Elitists and traditionalists might argue these canons have influenced the world for centuries or, at least, since the invention of print. Further arguments claim that these "great works" give us images, information, and interpretations of reality that have played a major part in the modern imagination. In fact, the novel, a literary invention of the modern age, is, according to Brooker (1992), "a privileged arena." What is forgotten is that the "canons," for that matter, any literature texts, are "[socially] generated" (Selden, 1993), which leads not to universals but to texts that are ever-changing throughout time and space. The "canons" of literature are placed in crisis; their meanings are not universal but become dominant, both in use and interpretation of reality.

Dominance includes knowledge and values that seek "to develop a totalizing theory that embraces the self, society, interaction, and even entire civilizations" (Denzin, 1992). This arrogance excludes texts of gender, race, class, and other differences, or, if including differences, places the representations in positions of helpless, powerless agencies. Even dramatic texts, scripts, and improvisational material are subject to literature in crisis.

Minority literature (including dramatic texts) from "the colonies" are good examples of the problem of the "canonization" of literature. As Fuentes (in Brooker, 1992) argues, "a sacred text is, by definition, a completed and exclusive text." The appropriation of international literature is political intervention. The tendency of the minority or colonial literature to write back to the imperial center, to create an imagination that still privileges the Western European worldview is also dangerous. In other words, the cultural constructions "ranging" from knowledge, values, institutional structures to subjectivities, even in the literature of "others," perpetuates the dominant view of the world, especially the master/slave, governor/governed, ruler/ruled concepts (Ashcroft, Griffiths, and Tiffin, 1989). Wa Thiong'o (1986), a Kenyan writer and dramatist, chose to stop writing in English and create literature only in his native language—a decolonizing of the mind—by writing away from the Empire.

Since literature carries ideology and no reader ever reads from a position of neutrality (Wright, 1989), texts are a source of cultural constructions as powerful as the dominance of mass media. Constructions of gender, class, sexuality, race, and social and political relationships can be easily excluded from interrogation if modern texts are seen as unarticulated, fixed meanings embedded deep within the narratives of literature—another crisis of modernity.

AUTHOR/ITY IN CRISIS

I wonder if today, in academic circles, there is a text (whether oral, printed, television, film, or other media) that does not quote or reference an expert's thoughts or words. This dependence on the "author"/ity of another's knowledge, words, and values that validates or legitimizes one's own "author-ity" is a crisis most frequently found in the culture of academia. Students, as well as professors, become slaves to the "authority of textbooks" (just check the university bookstores or photocopying bills for this phenomenon). "Experts" in the fields of disciplinary knowledge name-drop Foucault or Baudrillard (as I have done in this book) or claim "authorship" of abstract phrases such as "polyphony" (Bakhtin, in Holquist, 1990) or "seduction and hegemony" (Miller, 1990) and leave students who are impressed by authority intellectually marginalized.

In turn, the crisis is compounded by the demand for students or lay people to use esoteric language without any ground to their own lives or interests. In this way, the author's knowledge, truth, values, and cultural constructions remain, as legitimized and absolute. Essays, assignments, or projects are developed as the experts read and write/present/quote their ideas. The closer you match their language and thoughts, the better your marks. In one way, the traditional art of the essay is lost. For the past few decades, students have been required to read exhaustively, take lecture notes (developed by the professor, not photocopied), rework the ideas, and rewrite them to make them their own—in other words, become one's own "author-ity." Essays were valued, if indeed students and professors worked rigorously, consistently, and constantly to engage in a dialogue (both oral and written) that was valued if a student challenged, questioned, and interrogated the texts of others. This was perhaps an ideal in the past, a part of "author-ship. "

Foucault (oops, not practicing what I preach), embarrassed by his own attempts "to establish a genealogical table of exceptional individuals" [a list of authors to legitimate his thinking], questions the "status we have given the author . . . when we began our research . . . systems of valorization in which he was included . . ." (Foucault, 1977, p. 115). He calls the challenge to the "author-ity" of a text counter-memory, that is, "a memory that intervenes in history rather than chronicles it. In other words, counter-memory participates by interrogating; it does not accept the past "as it really was as written by the authorities" (Marshall, 1992, p. 50). Counter-memory also influences interpretation, rehearsal, intervention, and performance works in the dramatic arts. What is in crisis is the lack of counter-memory theories or strategies. Even the scripted or improvisational texts of the dramatic arts, camp skits, or classic canons of drama and creative dramatics are in a crisis of authority.

Another culprit in the unchallenged world of author-ity is writing as capital. As I put this pencil (my authorship technology) to paper, each letter or word is one ink mark closer to tenure or academic blackmail. I urge readers to cross out, cross over, write between the lines and in the margins challenges to my knowledge claims. The authors' individualistic concepts, words, structures, and values become a cultural commodity. Nowhere is this more evident than the culture of celebrity authors and aesthetic commodities among book-selling tours, autograph collecting, talk shows filled with mass-market authors, and university classes filled with the "authoritative" textbook. Authors sometimes become as celebrated as their books—authors such as Truman Capote, Henry Miller, Simone de Beauvoir, or Anaïs Nin. What they write about becomes less important than who they are. When I recently asked a literacy class of university students to question John Grisham's representations of women in his stories, it was as if I had asked the students "to take arms" against the author—an instant hero! The author, placed in the spotlight, is enabled by apolitical readers or spectators to maintain "regimes of reason" (Leitch, 1992, p. 36).

The major text in dramatic arts is presented orally, although it might have originally been a printed script. Whether the origins of dramatic texts are printed or oral, the process of rehearsal is the site where the author-ity of what is presented can be challenged. For women, the oral tradition for many centuries was the main source of information (midwifery, gossip, back fences, tea time), since access to print (given to men through education or careers) was denied. Ned Bear, a Maliseet Native American, claims that challenges to author-ity at the university level are still driven mainly by white, middle-class, Eurocentric men and women. His challenge to authority comes in his resistance to print. "White man won't believe anything unless it's in print or referenced" (Bear, 1994). And Barthes, a European writer, quotes Bear as an authority. "Writing is that neuter, that composite, that obliquity into which our subject(ivity) flees, the black-and-white where all identity is lost, beginning with the very identity of the body that writes" (Barthes, 1986, p. 49).

Author-ity/ship, a major source of social discourse that controls text and "compels us to think in certain ways" (Barthes 1986, p. 3) is, in modern life, in crisis. Authority in the dramatic arts spans the theoretical underpinnings of authors such as Aristotle, Artaud, Brecht, or Beckett, to the classical canons of Shakespeare, Moliere, Ibsen, Simon, or Sheppard, to acting strategies such as Stanislavski's. Challenges to authority is the task of future rehearsals and the burden of postmodern performances.

INDIVIDUALISM IN CRISIS

Who am I? and who are we? takes us into one of the major features of modern life in relation to those two questions. The crisis here is that the former has dominated the twentieth century under titles of existentialism, freedom of the individual, "do my own thing," "be my own person," and "to find myself." In each case, this centering masks the fact that the individual is as much constructed by social formations as it is by self. With this in mind, modern life has used individualism as a forum for a capitalist context, a seductive force for selling freedom as individual choice and diversion from the influence of social and cultural power upon individualism as actually constructed by subjectivity. Thus, the move would be toward a dismantling of individualism and toward a "circuit of capital . . . culture that captures the ways in which social relations of power, cultural forms [institutions and bureaucracy], and human subjectivities are intertwined" (Kelly, 1993, p. 3).

In modern life, the power of social structures (including history, representations, texts, institutions, knowledge, language discourse) that construct the individual has been left largely unchallenged or unquestioned. First, a genre of questions that adjudicates the "power of social structures" has yet to be formulated. Second, people of modern life, conditioned by history, modern mythologies, institutions, and, in the late twentieth century, by mass media and capitalism have little reason to change or disrupt the dominant cultural imperialism of the self over the subject as a social, cultural, and historical formation. The latter condition comes to be known as hegemony—that is, a world of power and dominance exists as it is left uninterrogated (to be discussed in more depth and greater variety in Chapter 5).

Traditional curriculum prompts students to view themselves as free individuals, while blocking any inquiry into the status of their freedom of choice between subject and individual (Myrsiades and Myrsiades, 1994, p. 39). Individualism, "as an object of exchange in an economy founded on heterosexual bourgeois familial relations and whose ideology is so determined to validate dominant culture" (Aston, 1995) (especially bourgeois, middle class), presents a complex pattern of social relations, which in turn becomes seductive and taken for granted.

In addition, "norms of interaction" (discourse) work to shape the self and continue the evolution of self-identity through the communicative interaction with others (Benhabib, 1992, p. 71). A way of talking and developing concepts becomes part of an identity logic that keeps the constitution of the individual privileged over the construction of the subject as an agent or as constituted by culture. Exclusions of certain identities become the norm, such as those of gender, race, class, sexuality, physical, mental, and spiritual difference, and also legitimize stabilizing claims of subjectivity as totalized and fixed.

One of Lyotard's (1989) claims about the modern subject in crisis supports Butler (1993) and others when he states how multiple constructions of subjectivity come up against the totalizing order of narrative, that is, the power of discourse to collect all subjectivity under (especially capitalism and Marxism) dominant theories that skirt identity politics.

Although the late modern age has turned attention to identity as subjectivity instead of individualism, certain subjectivities still take precedence, in theory and practice, over others. As Dolan argues: "Male sexuality is still active, privileged and displayed" (Dolan, 1993, p. 124). In any of the dramatic arts, to talk or present multiple intersecting identities and positions of subjectivity is difficult. The dramatic arts as agency for interrogation and disruption of subjectivity in crisis becomes an important site for exploration of modern constructions. A playful, ludic, risk-taking, creative environment is necessary, as well as practices informed by contemporary theories.

MARGINS IN CRISIS

Who lives in the margins? Where are the margins? If there are margins, must there be centers? Who decides what are margins or centers? How did margins come to be so? Does moving the margins to the center only create new margins and change the oppressors into the oppressed? Who profits from politics of the margins? What has happened throughout the process of modernization that has created "margins"?

Like other aspects of modern life, margins are created by a social apparatus in place in Western culture since the early Greek *polis* (state). It could be argued that as early as that time, state apparatuses placed women at the margins. Not only has their participation been nonexistent (according to most history books), the laws organized a society founded on women's suppression (Wiseman, 1989). Traditional patriarchal systems have relegated differences to marginal positions of nonsubject (when did women, Afro-Americans, Native Americans get the vote?), nonspeaking states of silence. Systematic exclusions that marginalize through difference become a metaphor for modern life.

The margins are everywhere—exclusion based on differences exist where the privileged are the dominant and at the center, or the homeless on the fringe. Everywhere in our world, there are margins; in text, representations, values, knowledge, institutions, history, subjectivities, and a host of other locations. "The center becomes powerful and creates a state of marginality" (Kelly, 1993, p. 23).

Then the backlash. Collective consensus that defines the margins systematically excludes the other through history, discourse, and institutional practices. In other words, the center creates phobias, legitimates itself, and articulates the policies and legislation that maintain and control the margins. A selective prejudice emerges almost to the point of rituals that lose the meaning of political struggle to that of decentering and blurring centers and margins—a hegemonic state.

At the end of the modern period (assuming we are there or past it), the margins have become "an unprecedented source of creative energy . . . an impetus towards decentering and pluralism" (Ashcroft, Griffiths, and Tiffin, 1989, p. 12). Within the context of the dramatic arts, sensitivity to the margins and the challenge to dismantle the centers and chart the voyage of the margins to the center becomes the task of participants and spectators alike.

BORDERS IN CRISIS

The recent dismantling of the Berlin Wall is a metaphor for the dismantling of borders in the late twentieth century. National borders as well as conceptual borders of knowledge, values, disciplines, and traditional borders of mythology, history, literary genres, representations and institutions are being dismantled, mainly in theory more so than practice. Before I problematize the crisis of borders and the implications of border-crossing, especially for the dramatic arts, I would like to discuss how borders are culturally constructed and how they match constructions of modern life.

Borders contain, limit, control, maintain, frame, separate, divide, segregate, protect, include, and exclude. The Berlin Wall was a politically constructed border that separated ideologies and nationalities while containing and controlling ideologies within each of its borders. I say *borders* because not only did the wall separate East and West Berlin, but it contained ideologies of America, Britain, and France—all of which were contained within East Germany. These borders limited movement of ideas, economy, families, information, and so on, to only that which was acceptable within each of the boundaries determined mainly by Western powers.

True borders work when the members agree to use common symbols (Kershaw, 1992) (including those of language) without any great degree of conflict or dissension (mind you, in the case of Berlin, dissension meant death, institutional isolation, or excommunication). Where intellectual or conceptual borders exist between ideologies, theories, value, or knowledge, the creation of epistemological disciplines emerge, and, over time, become locked within their own borders, excluding outside ideas or frameworks. Subject disciplines in educational circles, especially university, are more and more exclusive and separated from one another. Modern life is the age of specialists defined mainly by the "expert" knowledge one possesses. Disciplinary borders prevent access between different interests and expertise.

Borders, whether national, epistemological, international, or local, whether based on gender, race, class, age, sexuality, or other differences, discriminate and exclude subjectivities, knowledge, values, behavior, history or representations that do not match or conform to the collective complexion. This crisis of borders has implications for the dramatic arts. Here, the playful, creative nature of the border-crossing and blurring between content, form, genre, time and space, otherness, and body as site can occur. Dramatic arts have been playing at the margins and cross-borders for centuries. The dominance, however, of bourgeois, Western dramatic theory and practice has excluded any other notions of the dramatic arts that do not work within these borders. In the future, to overcome the crisis of borders, the dramatic arts will need to develop theories and practices that are culturally inclusive, first by recognizing how borders limit or exclude and how border-crossings, like centering the margins, add creative energy and thought, both to process and performance.

DRAMATIC ARTS IN CRISIS

Western philosophy, since its birth in early Greece, has provided various ways to reflect on and structure the world, including ways of thinking about and doing dramatic arts. The dramatic arts, needless to say, like the history of the Western world, has its roots in the early Greek theater. Since those days, dramatic renderings of reality and fantasy have changed over the course of time: from medieval to renaissance drama, to modern renditions such as Brechtian epics, Theater of the Absurd, minimalist theater, performance theater, to the current technological gala approaches of popular and musical theater. Each format, as a symbolic representation, shapes reality differently in accord with or as a question about the prevailing philosophical structures of the time.

The dramatic arts are shaped by and reshape the world. The focuses of dramatic arts change through time, and the context depends upon what and whose needs are being served. Drama has been used for many purposes: aesthetics, creativity, politics, cultural dissemination, advertising, catharsis, therapy, performance, interpretation, social learning, and, to the present-day supremacy, of "pure" entertainment. In large part, these different positions and purposes govern the uses, practices, audiences, and studies to which drama attends. In this book the concern is how the history of Western theater links to the history of educational drama.

A history of the dramatic arts in education is reviewed by Bolton (1979). Briefly, he describes the history of educational drama as located in three distinct arenas, each one connected in some oblique way to the philosophical and historical foundations of Western theater. The most common type is, of course, the school theater production, philosophically derived and adapted over the centuries from Greek theater. The second format has been the creative movement/therapy/theater games/improvisation format advocated mainly by Peter Slade in Britain and Viola Spolin in the United States, descended mainly from the theoretical techniques of Stanislavski. Finally, and perhaps the least commonly used or understood perspective of educational drama, is group-process drama or social-learning drama; fostered theoretically by Brecht (with a Marxist text on his desk!) and practiced creatively by Heathcote (in O'Neill, 1984) and politically by Boal (1985). Crucial to the context of this book is how each of these domains cross borders in addition to the impact and implications of cultural studies and criticism for educational drama.

Whichever type of drama dominates the curriculum, any one of them is in crisis. Modern dramatic arts are generally, especially within school contexts, ideologically conservative. All forms and content of the dramatic arts, although potential agents for changing reality, tend to "be distorted by ideologies" (Wright, 1989, p. 24) supported by bourgeois capital, where formalist analysis and performances are reproductions of the dominant cultural knowledge valued by modern-day constructions. Modeled on the bourgeois alleyways of New York and London, school-based dramatic arts remain politically neutral, promote an essentially conservative curriculum, maximize the dramatic arts as therapy, "acquiesce the dominant culture's desires" (Dolan, 1993, p. 49), and privilege the authority and dominance of the traditional canons. Each of these areas work from exclusionary models that absent the margins and voices of contradictions.

The dramatic arts, based on inclusionary theories and practices (not purely as social issues, but political action), would be responsible for "mobilizing a certain critical consciousness" (Boyne and Rattansi, 1990, p. 202) within any dramatic context that allows teachers and students to engage processes and strategies that intervene in the norm and produce disturbances in "cultural constructs and the means of cultural production" (Kershaw, 1992, p. 5). Dorothy Heathcote and Augusto Boal are two major educators who have moved beyond formalist analysis. The former works with mythological, distancing, and anthropological realms (such as teacher-in-role and mantle of the expert), and the latter works explicitly with the political theories of Marxism and the strategies of Western realism and drama therapy (forum theater, Theater of the Invisible, and legislative theater). Theater based on inclusionary practices (including gender, race, etc.) would need "to take into account all aspects of the event [contexts] which bear on the ideological transactions" (Kershaw, 1992, p. 23).

EDUCATION IN CRISIS

From a cultural studies and criticism position, all aspects of education are in crisis. Dominated by a conservative, apolitical curriculum, teachers, students, knowledge, and values are confined by a profession that "perpetuates limiting world views" (Agger, 1991, p. 90). Left unchallenged are worldviews about what constitutes knowledge, truth, subjectivity; whose and how histories are to be told; how representations and subjectivities are constructed in historical and political contexts; how discourse shapes how and what we know as well as whose discourse is dominant (science, arts, male, white, heterosexual?). Teachers and students remain in a professional class instead of "transformational intellectuals" (Myrsiades and Myrsiades, 1994, p. 43).

"For the entrenched powers" (Caputo, 1987, p. 194), cultural constructions based on differences (gender, race, etc.) are a threat. Changes in curriculum objectives, content, purposes, teaching, learning, materials, and revaluations are disruptive—economically, politically, and pedagogically. Educators and curriculum, lodged in traditional modes of thinking, avoid challenge and struggle (myself included) against exclusionary theories and practices due to a host of seductive forces (such as paychecks, certification, public outcries, and the peacefulness of not "rocking the boat"). Educators and curriculum, however, as potential agents of change, through interrogations and disruptions of unchallenged cultural constructions, can begin the process of dismantling curricula and themselves.

DON'T DESPAIR

To begin with, this book is not criticizing the world from an existential angst where the individual is living in some kind of personal hell, a state of despair or hopelessness. It assumes the world is in a mess not because of individual mistakes, faults, or sin but because of larger, more illusive realms than that of mere individual existence. Contemporary theories of cultural studies and criticism provide us with a language and a structure to "see" the world, interpret and understand the world, and perhaps change how it is or how it has always been. The crisis—the mess—has been constructed by social, economic, political, historical, and cultural apparatuses much larger than an existential (supposedly free choosing) individual can muster. Definitely, however, the crisis did not occur by "natural" circumstances. Organizational structures, created over time by social groups (not individuals)—since the beginning of human time—have contributed profusely to this crisis.

As a theoretical introduction to rehearsals of cultural descriptions, this chapter may seem rather despairing, with tones of Armageddon and hopelessness about our world. The intention, however, is not to create despondency about the future or nostalgia for the past. With a sincere desire to "get on with it," the themes of modern life "in crisis" assume an initiation ritual for the interrogation and dismantling of modern life through contemporary theories and practices of cultural studies and criticism through the dramatic arts.

Awareness about the conditions of modern life believed to be in crisis by the theoretical lens of cultural studies and criticism has been presented in this chapter. Major themes are discussed ranging from knowledge, truth, history to homogenization, subjectivities, and discourse. Of course, the major themes in crisis bring us into the world of postmodern theory, deconstructionism, poststructuralism, and postcolonialism. One of the first premises with which artists must work is to agree that the theory and dramatic arts approaches they encounter are a means of interrogation. Strategies presented in Chapter 6 challenge cultural constructions, not as a neutral or natural world, but as a world inhabited by humans who structure what the world is, has been, or could be.

PRACTICAL SUGGESTIONS

1. Upon entrance into the dramatic arts class or sessions, hand each student/participant a file card with a key word from Chapter 1. Have them work in pairs and perform a one-minute scenario for another pair, first in mime, then with dialogue. Guess what the key word is. Switch pairs.

2. Upon entrance, hand a file card with a key word on it from Chapter 1, and a pin to each participant. Without revealing what the word is, have each participant pin the card on someone else's back. Everyone will have a mystery word on her or his back. The participants can ask each other questions that can be answered only with a "yes" or a "no." This continues until the participants can correctly guess the word pinned on their backs.

3. Write each of the major themes of crisis mentioned in Chapter 1 on a separate piece of large chart paper or separate overhead sheets. Have the students brainstorm an everyday, concrete example of the crisis either from the imagination, reality, popular culture or media, literature, or history that could be portrayed in a minute and half scenario.

4. Have a group of four to six participants create an everyday common ritual (e.g., one that occurs in family routines, churches, schools, with friends, in different contexts, military hospitals, clinics), one minute in length, that is taken for granted as a "natural" part of modern life. Have one group perform the ritual, after which the audience discusses what theme of Chapter 1 the ritual represents. Is it a construction of modernity or not? How?

CHAPTER 2

Cultural Studies through Theater

CULTURAL STUDIES

In what way could an area of studies be developed that would address the crisis of modern life yet not, in itself, be constructed as repeating or continuing the crisis? One major area has become known as cultural studies. As a contemporary influence, "cultural studies" has become an umbrella term for a host of theories and practices that attempt to challenge and surpass the various crises of modern life without assembling the same patterns and structures as those originally interrogated and dismantled. Cultural studies gathers under its umbrella several theories and practices; sometimes the distinctions between them are clear, at other times, blurred. The major theories under the rubric of cultural studies are deconstructionism, postcritical theories, postmodernism, poststructuralism, postcolonialism, and now, postliteracy and postfeminism have joined the discussions and debates. Although each theory has distinctive features and approaches, there are common themes that thread through the discourses. The most foregrounded theme is power and how it plays itself out in the cultural constructions of truths, knowledge, discourses, history, literature, subject disciplines, and institutions. Inherited, perhaps, from Marxist and feminism theories, these "post" theories partner well with the dramatic arts as tools for interrogation and dismantling of cultural constructions that exclude, marginalize, silence, and operate in our everyday lives. Since there are excellent introductions and extensions to these contemporary theories in other books and journals, I will discuss only some of the key points of the theories. The task that remains is to connect these theories to implications for theories and practices in the dramatic arts.

I will suggest the general aspects of cultural studies' potential impact on dramatic arts. The latter's format provides a space for rehearsing radical changes in the who and what of culture constructions that traditionally, especially the content and structures of modernity, have excluded the voices of the margins, the invisible and the silent. The purpose of this book overall is to bring critical cultural studies and the dramatic arts into dialogue; in the long run, to evoke critical thinking practices in our everyday lives.

The word "cultural" usually conjures up a variety of images and definitions. One university student who asked about my course titled Cultural Studies through Theater thought drama, in a cultural studies class, meant studying and presenting scripted plays of different countries and ethnic groups. Culture, like drama, is a "signifying system through which a social order is communicated, reproduced, experienced and explored [including] . . . relations of gender, class, race, etc. . . . representations of real social relationships" (Kelly, 1993, p. 7). Who and what is marginalized or invisible within these two signifying systems (culture and drama) need to be presented; hegemonic practices need to be interrogated and dismantled by the performers and spectators.

Cultural studies raise new sets of questions and present the possibility for new sets of critical practices that, in turn, encourage awareness and potential agency for reconstructive practices that might not cure the crisis but, at least, incur change in the thoughts and attitudes of participants and spectators of the dramatic arts. Caution is suggested, however, against simply restating cultural formations rather than mounting a genuine critique of resistances and alternative actions. We must not place ourselves outside but must infiltrate the structures of culture. As agents, we need to remain grounded in everyday reality, yet illuminate power and exclusions through artistic practices. We fail to interrogate and disrupt modern cultural constructions if we merely restate.

Cultural studies itself can be "in crisis." As with modern life, to repeat the constructions that led to the crisis in the first place is dangerous. Similar to Barthes (1986), who claims that his autobiography would be written as a challenge to his own ideas, the same is true for cultural studies when incorporated into any of the dramatic arts. Cultural critics never seem to avoid reaching comfortable positions or sediment in their own ideas. In dramatic contexts, inequality, marginality, and exclusion are not mere abstractions. Actors, students, directors, and others engaged in rehearsing cultural interrogation and disruptions through dramatic arts must eventually reflect on themselves—a terrifying and risky business.

Cultural studies in itself is a cultural construction embedded potentially with the very same crisis as modern life. Panaceas question, challenge, direct, focus, and change cultural formations. At the same time, they can be totalities, fixed grand narratives, dominant and exclusive of anything other than themselves. Cultural studies workers are aware of this dialectic and claim no closure on any challenges, resistances, directions, thoughts, or actions. Dramatic arts are initially (at least in theory) "labor" intensive in thought, body, action, and spirit. The added dimension of cultural studies puts the dramatic arts in constant process, where products lack capitalistic, bourgeois intention or modernistic closure, that is, everyone could live happily, comfortable but not unequal to or dominated by others.

Dramatic arts theories and practices, informed by cultural studies, can offer possible, real, everyday resistances and alternative formations. They offer agency for variations on taken-for-granted cultural constructions that are marginalizing and exclusive of different voices, experiences, and histories that do not fit with the dominant, powerful, colonial structures (such as institutions, representations, discourses) of everyday life.

Neither can cultural studies turn to method or technical strategies. Caputo (1987) speaks of radical hermeneutics as keeping the question of "being" open. Indeed the task of hermeneutics is seen as radical in its resistance to methodological thinking. He echoes Heidegger's (1977) resistance to reducing "thinking" to technique or method, a dominant element of modern life (witnessed by the plethora of self-help technical books and textbooks). Radical hermeneutics, like the dramatic arts, does not depend on method for acting, directing, and scripting, although this has been a traditional practice evidenced in Stanislavski method acting, theater games, and creative dramatics—strategies that belong to both mainstream theater and educational drama.

Clarification of what constitutes cultural studies is multidimensional and multilayered. Although there are several positions in cultural studies, the one consistent characteristic has "been a sense of critical political involvement—in particular, a desire to understand and change structures of dominance in industrial capitalist societies" (Blundell, Shepherd, and Taylor, 1993, p. 3). With the key words being "dominance," "understand," and "change," an examination of the world through a cultural studies lens ranges "in a broad anthropological sense [to] any expressive activity contributing to social learning" (Agger, 1992, p. 2), that is, text.

"Expressive activity," as outlined by Agger and with implications for drama, includes:

1. *Political and intellectual agenda.* For drama, this means practices that are intellectually informed by cultural studies and criticism theories. These practices are intended for recognition and transformation of society's content and structures and are concerned with power structures that exclude. If we, as drama educators, are serious about equity and justice in all aspects of our curriculum, then everything from scripted texts to the drama-play center in kindergarten are subject to the intellectual and political agenda of cultural studies.

2. *Political intervention.* Once oppressive content and structures are identified, dramatic rehearsal processes offer alternatives, rerouting and changing the course of oppression, at both the individual and the societal level. Mere reenactment is not the goal. Rather the outcome is the creation of a concrete repertoire of strategies and policies that may, as in the case of Boal's work (1985) with Brechtian Lehrtheater (learning/teaching-play theater), claim intervention as "a series of social, political, and ideological interruptions that remind us that representations are not given but produced" (Boal, 1985, p. 19).

3. *Challenge to familiar and taken-for-granted knowledge.* Perhaps one of the more difficult tasks of doing dramatic arts, driven by cultural studies, is to have participants recognize oppressive structures or people. Students often claim that "it is meant to be"; "that is the way it has been done in the past"; "it is tradition." Nietzsche (1980) regards this as an abuse of history, that is, holding onto the familiar and assuming it is natural. Althusser (1972) and Gramsci (1973) call the acceptance of dominant ideology "hegemony"; that is, "the ruling groups maintain their power and their control over the social system because the majority accept their predominance as the norm" (Kershaw, 1992, p. 19). Intervention, or to change what is not recognized or accepted as in need of change, is the burden. The field of habit, rituals, traditions, and history must be subject to a critical unpacking of the God-given. In other words, theater can serve as a site for the uncovering of oppressive cultural constructions.

4. *Subjects as their own cultural and historical creators.* We are objects of ideological production and creations of our own

sociocultural history. The important point to keep in mind is that once dramatic processes reveal the intolerableness of social realities, participants are responsible for "rehearsing" alternative choices and actions that move toward transformation, that is, intervention in the process of construction of our worlds. Subjects become agents of change.

5. *Culture as conflict over meaning.* Cultural studies theory offers alternative formations to assign value to human existence, expression, and experience. In a culture where men do the tasks of cooking and childrearing and the women are the hunters, it is the domestic world that is assigned more value—culture is gendered. Dramatic arts, from a cultural studies perspective, are neither role reversal nor doing dramas about oppressed people. It is about creating strategies to structure the world that let us "resee" undervalued individuals and groups in order to elevate them to positions of privilege (not just economically but socially, culturally, politically, and so forth). This reassignment of privilege and value fits with one of the major arguments of postmodernist theory: for a pluralist and decentered competition of cultures and ideologies, within a society which has a multiplicity of orders in constant conflict with each other, thus precluding the possibility of a dominant ideology (Kershaw, 1992, p. 20). The playfulness and possibilities of dramatic arts offer an exploratory but safe site for disclosures of inequities, voicelessness, powerlessness, and injustices. In addition, dramatic arts interaction between the real and the imaginary and the audience's collective imaginative interpretations of the staged action encourage the construction of alternative worlds.

6. *The impact of popular culture.* One of the major influences upon the movement from modern to postmodern theater has been that of popular culture. Images, icons, and structures in popular literature and media (television, film, videos, and CD-ROM) produced for mass consumption are a major influence on the way we structure ideas and ways of life. The impact has permeated every aspect of education including social relationships. One of the major causes of violence, as we tend to think, among school students, is attributed to the images that they see on television and in the movies. No longer is the family or the school the center of education. bell hooks (1990) states: "responding to televised cultural production, black people could express rage about

racism as it informed representation" (1990, p. 4), that is, the construction of images. Popular culture is a seductive way of influencing the mind.

7. *De-disciplining intellectual methodologies.* Most of us, from early school to university, have been socialized into education by disciplined specific knowledge, most commonly through mathematics, literature anthologies, science, history, and even art and drama textbooks. As early as grade one, students' learning is time-tabled according to bodies of disciplined knowledge. It is relevant to note that at the university level, learning continues to be organized around faculties such as arts, science, business, with a hierarchy of courses defining intellectual specializations even further. At any level of learning, knowledge is selected, organized, and presented as legitimate, valid, established, hierarchical, and intellectual (Foucault, 1972).

The most dominant authority on thinking and practice is the scientific method. Gadamer (1982), in *Truth and Method,* follows a line of thinkers who claim that one does not necessarily arrive at the truth to a question through method. The scientific method with its empirical renderings eliminates the cultural context (social, cultural, historical, political, and economic) in which questions are asked and answers are found. Kuhn (1970), in *The Structure of Scientific Revolutions,* and Watson (1968), in *The Double Helix,* show that no scientific explanation or discovery takes place in a decontextualized environment; even the method is controlled by external factors that influence not only a line of thinking, but the process by which findings are made known.

POSTMODERNISM

When Bronwyn, at age ten, went shopping for a gift for her mother, she claimed emphatically to the store clerks, "It has to be POSTMODERN!" Years later, the term appears increasingly in academia, literary journals, cocktail parties, and even the occasional situation comedy (*Seinfeld*) or advertisements (Sprite's synchronized swimmer-motor bikers). Perhaps Bronwyn still understands better than we do.

Today, one of the most prominent words appearing in current philosophical and theoretical debates is "postmodernism." Discussions about the prefix "post" have been attached to the words "critical," "structural," "modern," and "colonial." Before we discuss the implications of "postism" of these areas, we need to discuss the roots of the words "critical," "structural," "modern," and "colonial."

Cultural studies discourse (as in this book) is about the position of subjects in relation to the objects of our world such as images and institutions. The major question is who in this context is being oppressed, marginalized, devalued, or colonized? One of the major areas that added knowledge to the field by asking similar questions was feminist theory. Feminist theories, women's studies, and gender studies have focused on questions of oppression and marginalization based on sexual constructions. Questions can reveal that there is, indeed, oppression, marginalization, or invisibility based on gender. The aim is to reconstruct the world so that exclusions do not occur, thus directing our thinking into a postmodern world. In other words, once we are aware of the structures that oppress or marginalize individuals or groups based on gender constructions, then we ask what actions do we take to illuminate these structures, images, or institutions? How do we restructure the world to move us into social equality and individual justice for all? The same application of cultural studies would hold for constructions that are oppressive of individuals and groups based on race, class, religion, knowledge, values, history, and a host of other cultural areas.

However, one must not be seduced into thinking that the postcritical world has arrived. In fact, the power and dominance of men over women, whites over blacks, West over East, capitalism over socialism, Christians over Muslims, the lack of access to the world based on physical and mental differences demonstrates that we have yet a long way to go. We need only to look as far as our immediate everyday lives to see the measures of injustice. We access the world scene mostly through television, film, and contemporary communication systems. When we view the world through a cultural studies lens, we understand how things work and how human beings are oppressed. The project is how do we institute actions and structures that reorganize the world? The dramatic arts as cultural studies has a part to play in that reorganization and creation of actions that move us toward a postcritical world—a ludic dance with ideas and possibilities.

Obviously to discuss the principles of postmodernism, it seems necessary to understand dominant features of modernism. The definitions of modernism are scattered. There are, however, some shared features such as: the rise of the theoretical, technological, bureaucratic, objective rationalization of the world, individualization, and industrialization, Westernization, commodified capitalism, urbanization, and homogenization of cultural differences. Embedded within these features lie promises and practices of progress, wealth, and quality of life.

These promises of liberation, however, mask modes of oppression and domination (Kellner and Best, 1991, p. 3). Foucault (1972) criticizes modern rationality and institutions as sources of domination. Furthermore, he studies how institutions obscure the different and plural nature of the social field. He argues that our obsession with the rationalization of self, social orders, politics, economics, and institutions, from family to prisons, have blinded us to how these features, in fact, produce oppression. Marginalization and devaluing of women, peasants, and colonized people are only some of the failures in the modernization of the world. The problem with the theories of Foucault and others such as Deleuze, Guattari, and Lyotard is that we are not aware of the problematic situation of their theories when we are immersed in the experience itself. Reflection on the modern world uses the discourse of cultural studies and criticism to step outside modernity.

Lyotard (1989), one of the leading influences upon our definition of postmodernism, criticizes modernism as the failed project of the enlightenment period: the failure of rationality (defined mostly by Western white males), the prisons of grand narratives such as Marxism and capitalism, and, in education, the equal failure of the grand narratives of Kolburg, Cole, Tyler, Taba, and the ubiquitous Piaget. These latter discourses have defined the field by influencing both the content and structure of teaching and learning, curriculum theory, and moral, social, and intellectual development. As the East gains prominence in the world, politically, economically, and culturally, the grand narratives of the West are diminishing in power or seductively engulfing themselves.

Postmodernism was "born out of a generational refusal of the categorical certainties of high modernism" (Storey, 1993, p. 158), that is, the growing dissatisfaction with the elitism of high culture and the finality, staticness, and exclusion by the dominant discourses. In addition, the growing impact of popular culture (a concept with many layers of meaning and definitions) upon the construction of our world through mediums such as rock videos, film, and television has moved us into a postindustrial, postmethodical, poststructural world. The study of culture through theater comes mainly from the regions of critical, postcritical, structuralism, poststructuralism, modernism, and postmodernism theories. Recognition of the oppressive structures of modernism through dramatic conventions and structures can create a playful, hypothetical, fantastical world of "postisms."

It might be appropriate here to mention that none of the contemporary theories claim "an approach" or techniques except deconstructionism. The dramatic arts, however, have particular approaches and conventions that construct meanings and produce conditions of power. When cultural studies and dramatic arts unite as a site for cultural deconstruction and reconstruction, questioning (see Chapter 6) becomes the major "strategy" for critical interrogations and investigation by contemporary theories. One of the first major investigative theories belongs to postmodernism.

The apparatus of postmodern theory is not an approach or set of techniques per se but, again, a political stance in regards to problematizing modern life. Like other contemporary cultural studies areas, postmodernism rejects most, if not all, of the constructions of modernism, modernity, and modernization (see the discussion in Chapter 1). Fostered by discontent more so than contempt, postmodernism rejects the constitution of Western culture by Eurocentric domination that privileges universal truths (Western culture), while science and technology exclude or marginalize all other ways of knowing (epistemology) and being (ontology).

Similar to cultural studies, postmodernism engages cultural criticism and resists the exercise of power in any cultural construction. In other words, as cultural movements both apply a mode of questioning to investigate systems of power legitimized by certain ideologies and large-scale structures (such as modernism and consumer capitalism—see Chapter 6 for questions). Modernism, in its historical path of rationalizing and categorizing truth, knowledge (note the rise of disciplinary expertise and subjects), texts, values, and other cultural constructions, "frames culture within rigid boundaries that both privileges and excludes around categories [of differences] especially gender, race, class, ethnicity" (Myrsiades and Myrsiades, 1994, p. 17). Postmodernism sets itself against modern constructions by challenging and, in some cases, breaking with the formalism and classicism of certain kinds of knowledge and power.

While challenging and disrupting the taken-for-grantedness of everyday life, postmodernism checks its own boundaries, discourse, cultural constructions, and ideological principles. With this in mind, when applying postmodern theory to any of the dramatic arts, the application itself is interrogated. What is moved to the center as dominant truths, gender, representations, and so forth, when postmodernism dismantles modern text? What is legitimized in postmodern representations in the dramatic arts? How can the piece be rehearsed so power representations and oppressive

structures are shifted or balanced? What and who is supporting and as-
signing power?

The task for postmodernism is to construct questions and rehearsals that
reveal and challenge the continuation of taken-for-granted forms of oppression. As Dolan (1993) claims, postmodernist theory "breaks with realist narrative strategies, heralds the death of unified characters by decentring the
subject, and foregrounds conventions of perception" (p. 88). Rehearsals, set
in a postmodern arena, can be directed along lines of cultural plurality and
contingency. To begin, try mixing contexts and genres of narrative strategies
instead of relying on traditional dialogue borrowed from classical text or
everyday language. Second, try shifting the central characteristics of a dominant persona to the background and foregrounding the unexpected; pull from
the marginalized recesses of the character and re-present these characteristics as dominant. The break with narrative realism challenges and dismantles
stereotypes, decenters privileged notions, and, hopefully, arouses all the participants in the dramatic arts, including audiences, to action. The goal is not
to anger, but rather to decenter subjectivities so as to privilege the margins,
foregrounding different cultural discourses, truths, knowledge, representations, structures, and so forth. The intent of rehearsals informed by postmodernism is to interrogate and disrupt power struggles embedded in any
cultural construction.

POSTSTRUCTUALISM

There are, as you gather while reading in the field, similarities among the
different theories of cultural studies that lead to different practices and
structures in the dramatic arts. Some of these differences, however, are
so blurred, for example, between postmodernism and poststructuralism,
that the question remains: Why have different theories? If you remember,
postmodernism makes claims of challenging its own theoretical and ideological constitutions. Other contemporary theories under the rubric of
cultural studies serve as mirrors and checks against any one theory becoming dominant or unified. Intellectual rigor and political energy at
play is a structural feature of cultural studies and the dramatic arts rehearsal process.

Unlike cultural criticism, "structuralism is a theoretical method and
not a political position" (Storey, 1993, p. 69). Structuralism consists of a
variety of methods that, when applied to a text, context, image, or contained world, fixes the meanings and structures in history, time, place,
and meaning. For example, "once upon a time" and "they lived happily

ever after" are familiar, taken-for-granted structures that are so much a part of our lives that we follow the pattern of getting married, having babies, getting a house, and living happily ever after. Or so we think. On the surface, this pattern is not true; that structure does not work for most of the population of the world. It is a single interpretation, a single fixed meaning. The inclusion of a plurality of experiences cannot be done in one text. Even the Cinderella story can be moved out of fixed meanings and structures by the application of poststructuralist thought.

In a cultural text (drama, print, oral, etc.), what we change no longer has value. In fact, we challenge what is being valued, or what is foregrounded. If money or beauty were put to the background, something else would come to the foreground as being more valued. We would assume that we are not trying to devalue it; we are trying to bring something else forward to be valued, to be at the center. As an example, Walt Disney Studios attempted (a capitalistic agenda?) to represent Belle, in *Beauty and the Beast* (1994), as an intellectual woman by constructing her as a reader. Belle's interest in books became foregrounded. Disney attempted to push physical beauty to the background and foreground the intellectual reader as beauty. Not surprisingly, Belle's body still remained seductively curvaceous, emphasizing her breasts and thighs.

Unified subjects want unified theories and thus "explicit" structure. Evidence of this can be measured by the dependence on a proliferation of self-help books and the multibillion dollar industry of textbook publishing in which knowledge and technique are prepackaged. Even dramatic arts are dominated by texts of structure from play writing to acting, from set design to directorial strategies. It is not just the power of the packaged structuring of dramatic arts that is seductive but the implicit structuring of culture hidden deep within methodological crevices. Soon the "facilitation" (which means in French and Latin "to make easy") of learning and teaching in the dramatic arts, as in other disciplines, remains uncreative and, from a political stance, inactive.

The taken-for-grantedness of familiar and comfortable structures rests in culture constructions that sleep, like Rip Van Winkle, only to awaken to the same world. This dormancy is extremely problematic for poststructuralists. Unquestioned structures contain dominant interests that maintain, circulate, and reproduce cultural constructions and thus "contribute to forms of racism, sexism, class exploitation" (Myrsiades and Myrsiades, 1994, p. 43). Dominant structuring principles of society remain intact without a theoretical dismantling by a mode such as poststructuralism.

I realize that I am perhaps giving the theoretical constructs of post-structuralism a different slant than intended by the major theorists. Why? I am attempting to accomplish three major activities in cultural studies (poststructuralism in this instance) as applied to the dramatic arts. Without a doubt, interrogating and dismantling cultural constructions of power and dominance is the primary intention. Second, the application of these contemporary theories informs the dramatic arts processes of rehearsal and performance. Finally, I use the ideas of poststructuralism in order to open the logocentrism (or narrative structuring) of the dramatic form to possible new formulations. An example should help clarify what I mean.

In a course called Cultural Studies through Theater, I invite the participants (usually five or six in a group) to perform three-minute familiar fairytale structures. The audience is then asked to identify familiar cultural constructions. Stepparents, families, royalty, privilege, gender, class, race, duties, responsibilities, truths, rescue, heroes, villains—the possibilities are endless. The common elements and characteristics are evident; without changes in content or form over time and space, the fairytale constructions, until recently, have been left unchallenged. Current Disney animated films make "token" reconstructions. Representations of Belle in *Beauty and the Beast* as a scholarly, thinking woman with a book in hand are so minimal that every other element of the fairytale remains unchanged. Men still ogle her body; villains and fools keep their status, especially the men; village women are still portrayed as marginal, hysterical, jealous gossipers out to "catch the right man"—to tame him. The film is a corporate money-maker left unchallenged.

However, hidden in the studios of artistic creations are potential challenges and political acts of poststructuralism. Without the glare of Walt and the seduction of capitalism, questions and discussions interrogate in safety and creatively dismantle dominant representations, relationships, discourses, and institutional power. First, we identify representations of power in Red Riding Hood, Snow White, Princess and the Pea, and the host of other familiar fairytales. We question the structures that create, maintain, and circulate the power (hegemony). We negotiate with the character (in-role)—why do they think "so and so" has power? How did he or she obtain it? How do they keep it? (this question begins the unfolding of hegemonic power structures, the topic of discussion in Chapter 5). Why don't the characters challenge the powers or the system? Why do the students answer: "That's the way it's supposed to be," "That's the way it's always been," and "We can't change history." As we ask the questions, we put each one on file cards to be posted for review, as incentives for change—a prologue to poststructural rehearsals.

What follows becomes an informed political act. The participants are then required to rework the piece they presented. They rehearse based on the questions and discussions that preceded. Content and structures are dismantled. Reconstructions of the fairytale incorporate principles of poststructuralism and focuses of cultural studies; that is, they reveal and change familiar power structures. Participants are asked to deconstruct the fairytale "text." Rehearsals become strenuous, painful, and tenuous, a sign that changes in the familiarity of fairytale constructions are occurring, but more importantly, a challenge in the actions and thinking of the participants. Subsequent presentations of fairytales do contain changes. The changes I have observed, however, are mostly shifts in gender, sexuality, and class constructions (men instead of women in traditional roles) or the addition of a non-European. These shifts only cloak the power representations instead of displaying imaginary possibilities of reconstruction for inclusion and power balance. Nevertheless, we recognize them as a beginning and a forum for rehearsing poststructural thought.

What is gained is markedly measurable from the first "raw" presentation, through the informed discussions and subsequent rehearsal processes to the next "poststructural" presentation. Granted there is usually much anxiety, stumbling, linguistic stammering, empty pauses, and a lack of sustained in-role play. But in the openness of the dramatic rehearsal process and the security of a "play" environment where risk-taking and laughter occur, the climate of fear is lightened. With the lack of closure or disbelief in ultimate meanings—both features important to poststructuralism—rehearsals and presentations break with classic and formal aspects of structuralism. Informed participants work against power structures, offer strategies for change, and involve the complexity of their differing perspectives.

Discourse, that is, the language of power and oppression, is perhaps the hardest element to dismantle in any cultural text. Peeling away the embedded structuring devices of language, however, even something as common as the first and last words of a fairytale, identifies the language/discourse in poststructuralism that floats; that is, there needs to be a constant dismantling of linguistic tropes (figures of speech) instead of mere discursive practices, hegemony, or literal meanings of words.

The examples I use are varied and multiple, but ones that seem to forecast poststructuralist notions that are mainly floating linguistic signifiers that empower. For example, in the case of a rape victim, to say

"How can I help you?" still puts the power in the words of the speaker, "I." To re-work the discourse to "What do you need me to do right now?" gives the control of power back to the victim. Control is structured by the discourse—a strategy that changes who has power. Participants can "script," formally or informally, the discourse (on file cards or over-heads) that dismantles the dominant citadels of power such as family, school, church, military, industry, business, medical, and state bureaucracies (Benhabib, 1992, p. 78). Assumptions of power embedded in language, even in the taken-for-granted discourse of fairytales, can be challenged, dismantled, and opened to new formulations of content, structures, and other cultural constructions.

Method can cast a dark shadow on truth. Methodology permitted a position legitimized by the dominance of a technological world that, from a cultural studies point of view, ignores elements that structure individuals and social beings. Like most disciplines, the dramatic arts are entrenched in a body of knowledge derived from methods of how to arrive at the answers. One of the most predominant influences on theater and drama in education has been the methodological support provided by Stanislavski—in lay terms—method acting. Other theorists and practitioners, such as Artaud, have given authority as well to individual revelations. When methodologies give more precedence to the individual than to social situations, this in turn gives priority to an imperialistic use of theater and drama. The danger is in the fact that the individual is governed by larger sociopolitical, cultural, and economic institutions and, as Marx would delight in, the economic materialism of production.

In modern society, methodology has become an intellectual and cultural commodity that supposedly sheds light on our world but, in fact, only serves to eliminate a larger cultural context. Dramatic arts informed by a cultural studies position cannot risk an empirical perspective. What is given authority in cultural studies is purpose and context, not method. Several major shifts are important to cultural studies and, in turn, become important to include during rehearsal processes, improvisational scenes, and performance analysis. A major point is that any dramatic arts context or scripted text is subject to political interrogation of contemporary culture. Intentions to uncover hidden dimensions of power existing in character constructions is the goal. What made he or she this way in thought, action, and word? Who gives whom power? How? On what is the power based in plot constructions? How is the action, scene, relationships, or tension constructed so that it privileges some experiences and relegates others' experiences to the background, margins, or silences? Who initiates action based on gender, race, age, class, or other traditionally privileged backgrounds?

Many contemporary theorists and practitioners claim to be critical cultural workers, but this could mean a range of several different thoughts and actions both in the dramatic arts and in the everyday. Several colleagues and myself think of ourselves as professors in cultural studies, each of us working from traditional disciplines such as art, early childhood, literacy, health, drama, and other areas, each with a different interpretation, discrimination, and selection of what constitutes "critical." Each of us, however, investigates the enabling and oppressive conditions within cultural constructions. We assume, as Giroux, that the focus of the investigations is "to produce a social discourse that does not accept needless human suffering and exploitation" (Giroux, 1991, p. 47). The statement matches well with the purpose of the dramatic arts driven by cultural studies as a political art form.

Any dramatist employing cultural studies has a responsibility to examine every dimension of everyday lived experiences portrayed through the stories of cultural representations. Within these acts of everyday life exist "the most telling dimensions of social dissatisfaction and political struggle" (Kelly, 1993, p. 3). Nuances that lie embedded within the action of the dramatic forms without the theoretical tools of critical cultural studies could remain unidentified and unchallenged.

Minor acts of representation, for example, school concerts or skits, are subject to the laws of a cultural studies interrogation. For instance, a group of fourteen-year-old boys were presenting a skit about girls. Not only was the stereotyping rampant, the dressing in drag an insult, the body movements intimidating to girls, but the teachers thought the representations were humorous. Questioned by a critical theorist about the representations of women and gender-crossing behaviors, the teachers felt there were no problems with the skit. Furthermore, they felt that "that's the way it is and always will be." Without the theories of cultural studies, the boys, girls, teachers, and the skits remained unchallenged. Three years later, the school still performed similar works, and the teachers still remained satisfied with "the social order" represented by the "signifying system" of this particular dramatic art form (Eyre, 1994). Humor, parody, and irony are major strategies for dismantling cultural representations and forms, but then again, what are appropriate forms?

POSTCOLONIALISM

Under the cultural studies rubric, postcolonialism is the least familiar or least used of the contemporary theories, perhaps because of the position of imperialism and dominance of postmodernism and poststructuralism writers. Of Europeans and Americans, the former is the major colonizer of the early modern era and the latter is the major colonizer of late modern times. Small wonder the major voices of postcolonialism are from previously colonized nations and cultures, such as the Middle East (Edward Said), Guyana (Wilson Harris), Afro-America (Henry Louis Gates Jr.), and colonial populations of the Caribbean, Indian, Australian, South American, and aboriginal voices throughout the globe.

Postcolonial theories act as a challenge to the cultural constructions of the colonizers whose impositions and interventions have destroyed or changed the cultural aspects of the original population. Whether the colonizers moved peacefully or in battle, the function was still to dominate and control, that is, to take over for economic, national, regional, geographical, religious, historical, or social purposes. Neuman and Stephenson (1993) define colonialism as "an apparatus which constructs by means of the actual dispersion of power and its symbolic practices of both colonizer and colonized" (p. 12). Colonization and postcolonialism portray cultural constructions that are colonized; the major issue is how dramatic representations position the colonized and the colonizer. The discourse used to create, maintain, circulate, and reproduce positions of power and oppression (hegemony) is an additional problem.

Two terms used (based on the assumption that the major function of language is a means of power) in the discourse of postcolonialism are "abrogation" and "appropriation." Abrogation refers to the denial of the language of the colonizer as the imperial power over the means of communication in any institutional site such as family, school, church, or state. Without acceptance of the imperial discourse by the colonized, control or imposition of cultural constructions are impossible. Control or imposition may come through legislation or military force such as the case of British legislation of English as the dominant or, in some cases, the only language to be spoken—a monolinguistic nation with monoculturalism. In other circumstances, the force may be dressed in "Black Robes," where the seduction and fear of Christian gods converted colonized populations into religious and thus linguistic realms. The language in which the Bible was written became the dominant language. Today, several Native Americans talk of being beaten at residential schools for speaking their "native" language while also being beaten at home if they spoke it. English was the language of power at school and, the parents thought, at home. Denial was difficult. Abrogation meant a loss of power for the colonized and control of aboriginal culture by the colonizer.

Appropriation of cultural constructions, especially through discourse, is available to both the colonizer and the colonized—the center and the margin, respectively. In the initial stages of colonization, the colonized appropriated the discourse of the center, reconstituted it both as a means of gaining access to the center and also as a means of challenging the center. Incorporating words and structures of the imperialist language, mixing it with the language of the margins, was an effective device for accessing or denying the power of the center. This kind of appropriation dismantled or at least weakened, in political terms, imperial power.

Currently, appropriation refers to the use of cultural constructions and artifacts by the imperial center in order to gain recognition and capital, for example, the use of traditional music, clothing, or organizational strategies appropriated by the center as their own or without social, political, or economic recognition or sensitivity. Nonaboriginal people have been appropriating land, medicine, education, and food from Native Americans since the days of Columbus. Recently, symbols, talking circles, rituals, knowledge, communication, child-raising practices, narrative and literary structures, and humor are just a few of the cultural appropriations of native culture by the non-native, Eurocentric population. Such appropriation serves only to position the colonized in the margins again.

For decades, the dramatic arts have appropriated native legends and rituals, albeit with misrepresentation more so than representation, and contaminated the cultural constructions through rehearsal processes and performances. Other cultural artifacts, values, rituals, and so on continue to be appropriated. Afro-American knowledge, values, and other cultural aspects that have been incorporated into North American life have lost or distorted their authenticity or "organic" qualities, so much so that most of the Afro-American population would not recognize their cultural origins.

Since colonialism is a way of maintaining an unequal international relationship of economic and political power (Said, 1978), the modern era has been caught up in the apparatuses of empire and colony, colonization of land, truths, knowledge, values, margins, border areas, gender, race, class, and other cultural constructions, without political challenge. With the modern age in crisis (Habermas claims it is an unfinished project of the Enlightenment) or at an end (as postmodernists such as Lyotard, Baudrillard, and others hope), the major means of challenge and change, peacefully we hope, is coming from the dismantling theories known as postcolonialism. Theoretical influences of postcolonialism interrogate modern cultural constructions, especially the history and systems of colonization and subject constructions of "other" by the colonizers.

Presentations of colonial encounters through dramatic arts usually appear in first renderings as an accurate account of reality—of how it is or how it was. In one scenario, students, mostly of European descent, depicted a news report on the killing of female babies in China as a means of population control. The depiction was then deconstructed for the power systems within the scenario. As the unpacking of the power dimensions began, I pointed out that most of the questions and discussion positioned the Chinese in a powerless, marginalized location, given that the site from which the questions emanated was the privileged position of students of European descent. The students felt colonialism was not an issue but that the "human injustice" of killing female babies was. Emotional rationale came into play, and it was difficult to dismantle the Euro-American position. Why, I asked, would China resort to this? Why female? Whose births? If you were Chinese, what options would you have? The discussion ranged from how wrong the killing was to some movement of the center to the margins—in this case decentering Euro-Americanism to value the margins. It was not necessary to judge the scenario as right or wrong but to reposition the interpretation and to give a sense of power to the margins. However discursive the arguments, killing female babies is wrong was the end position of the students.

This scenario is just one possibility for using postcolonial theory in the dramatic arts. Using newspaper or magazine stories is a way to begin the process of investigation of crisis created by colonialism. Scenarios of the Gulf War, peacekeeping in Bosnia, aid to Somalia, or other representations whether printed, visual, auditory, or otherwise are a good starting point for concrete examples of colonialism, especially as constituted by Europe and America. Select an article from a newspaper or magazine on events, issues, or circumstances in other places reported by a local or national writer/reporter. Present the scenario, either the actual event as reported or other possible contexts that surround the event, immediately or in the past. For example, an article on Bosnia could be depicted, not as at the scene, but as a family watching television on the report and then discussing it, or soldiers in a barracks being given a report by a commander, or other scenes in which the article is the content and the context is not that of the report. As the scenario unfolds, the audience can begin to interrogate, deconstruct, and challenge the representations of: Who is *really* in power? How is the power given to the Europeans or Americans and not to the Bosnians? Who benefits from this war? How could Americans stay out or resist? How is Bosnia colonized? What discourse of colonialism legitimates different actions by different groups? From what institutions, that is, military, church, business, United Nations, was power given, determined, circulated, maintained? What and whose representations are being seen as truthful, powerful, ethical, valued? Why? How are Bosnian culture constructions being represented that show oppression needing rescue from non-Bosnian parties? How could the reports be re-sisted/challenged by lay people, by military, by big business, by media? What shape would a rehearsal of the original scenario be like if decon-structed and reconstructed in a manner giving power to the victims? What positions do or do not contest the dominant European or American interpretations of the war?

This is just one scenario of colonialism interrogated by postcolonial theoretical questions. Hypothetical perhaps, but intended to show how the hidden, multiple layers of colonial power are exposed by the theoretical interrogations of postcolonialism. The questions themselves must be challenged as constructions that favor seeing the scenario with certain theoretical eyes. Cultural studies theories acknowledge their own political intent and stance, a challenge to its own ideology. As Said (in Williams and Williams, 1993) points out, historical interpretations, understanding, discourse, and action about, in, and for colonized populations "guarantee a position of superiority for the Westerner [colonizer] vis-à-vis the Orient as [other]" (p. 4).

Other areas of cultural studies use the trope (figure of speech) of col-onization to apply to cultural practices. Some feminist perspectives use the trope of colonization of the body by the medical profession, men, ad-vertising, art, and other carriers of culture. In the case of women, post-colonialism encourages the disruption of the control by others over their bodies—from representations in art, to abortion and surgery.

Wherever systems of power dominate, rehearsals that challenge these systems could benefit from the troping of colonialism/postcolo-nialism with sites other than just historical, geographical, economical or political. The female body as a site of colonization is just one example. Extend this trope to modern constructions of gender, race, class, sexual orientation, students in schools or university, or other categories and the possibilities are limitless. As "cultural recuperation" (Ashcroft, Griffiths, and Tiffin, 1989, p. 33) is, I assume, a major direction for postcolonial-ism, I have indeed barely touched the broader and more complex aspects of the theoretical implications for everyday practice or as an agency in dramatic arts performances.

CHAPTER 3

Major Tenets of Cultural Studies

FOREGROUNDING THE QUESTION

A fundamental resource of cultural studies is "the question." Questions both interrogate and disrupt. Through whatever mode they are presented, questions are the keys to using cultural studies in the dramatic arts—whether representations through body, discourse, institutional structure, histories (autobiographical and biographical), staging, lighting, blocking, acting, scripted or nonscripted material before, during, and after the rehearsal or performance.

Why, when, and how they are asked depends on from what theoretical position and for what purpose they are asked. What enables questions to be asked of what formations? What are questions that deconstruct, challenge, dismantle formations in crisis? What questions evoke resistance to hegemonic practices? What questions are not being asked? Why? What questions interrogate themselves or the answers generated?

Dramatic arts processes and/or performances (once they are in progress, beginning even with ideas to be performed or scripted) question cultural constructions that impede or at least slow down any attempts to proceed without challenge. Young children performing improvisations or storylike theater in the garage or classroom could be interrupted in their "play" with questions that ask them to reconsider the cultural formations they are portraying. Questions like Alyssia's "Why do the boys always get to be heroes?" could be asked as an aside during or after the performance by an aware adult: Why do the poor ones in the play always lose out to the rich? Why are rich people always powerful? Why do heroes all look the same? Cultural-studies-type questions inserted into the dramatic context, over time and space, make the play or performance a site for nurturing future cultural critics.

Interventionist forms, such as questioning, need to be foregrounded in the dramatic arts processes. The agent (e.g., teacher, director, actor, designer) and the agency (dramatic arts and cultural studies) work together to intervene, interrogate, and challenge both the constructions of cultural meanings represented by the dramatic art form and also the practices inherent in the dramatic art form itself. Each of the two processes serves as a check on the other—an interrogation of the interrogators.

Myrsiades and Myrsiades (1994) extend interrogation by questions to include the authority of institutions and disciplines. They claim that institutional structuring influences and positions students "so they are simply reproducing imaginary power relationships" (p. 123). The same could be said of the authority of dramatic arts practices. Simple opposition to the cultural constructions presented in a scenario might be actually reproducing and, in fact, legitimizing power relationships already well entrenched in the thoughts and attitudes of the students. Without a sense of what questions will dismantle power relationships within the contexts and texts (scripted and improvised) of the dramatic content and form presented, no productive opposition can take place.

Questions should ask what constitutes productive resistance. What are the elements that constitute nonresistance? What questions would dismantle the power relationships to expose how they oppress and marginalize differences? (See Chapter 6 for a list of questions and cultural studies text talk.)

Akin to recognizing power relations within a scenario or text, questions direct attention to the forms that constitute differences. Whether differences in truths, knowledge, values, representations, or discourses, questions seep through the cracks of a scenario, context, or text and reveal the differences based on gender, class, and other cultural constructions. In other words, if truths are being produced and accepted within a scripted or improvised scene, whose truths and knowledge are they? male? heterosexual? working class? Afro-American? colonizer? colonized? How did they get to be this way? How, why, and when were they culturally constructed?

Constant questioning of the imaginative world of dramatic art forms is a rehearsal for interrogations and disruptions of power relations in actual life. The questions of the cultural studies ilk, however, are not always foregrounded or valued in different contexts or times due to the acceptance by untutored subjects of the coherency, unity, and status of dominant positions or ideologies.

The Theater of Realism tends to mirror social/cultural formations instead of challenging reality. Locked into modern theater's obsession with the escapism of shallow fantasy and desires, fueled by modernism's structuring of desires as commodity, questions that challenge and change exclusionary practices are hazardous to box-office profits and dominant curriculum resources.

Brecht, a master at challenging modern cultural constructions through theater strategies, developed interventionist strategies that not only broke traditional theatrical formats but put the spectator in the position of questioning his or her own existence (Wright, 1989). Certain interventionist strategies such as the V effect, or displacement of "normal" acts, would, like certain critical questions, locate participants and spectators between the dominant centers and the silenced margins effecting a dismantling, questioning, and conflict with old beliefs about truth, knowledge, race, gender (although apparently Brecht was not sensitive to issues of race or gender). Dramatic arts, used in this manner, serve a political purpose.

Thus, dramatic processes become very important as a means to "redirect questions and thus answers" (Boyne and Rattansi, 1990, p. 189). The intervention of questions or strategies cultivated by cultural studies and criticism challenges traditional apolitical structures and knowledge of oppression, the aspects of life in crisis, and gives new meaning to the term "legitimate arts." Questions combine to do what any art does, that is, illuminate a situation, see it differently (even comically or absurdly), and more importantly, raise contentious questions about social and cultural contradictions. On the other hand, questions can barricade us into worlds that were meant to be dismantled. Within the play space of any dramatic art form, intervention is compulsory, either before, during, or after the action, but one must be careful of the kinds of questions that dismantle and those that perpetuate unchallenged (hegemonic) practices.

The point of using cultural studies questions as a disruptive strategy "inserts us into chaos, turmoil, the contingent, the discontinuous, and the unrepresentable" (Caputo, 1987, p. 187). Furthermore, questions that push the play into deeper investigation bring about a major shift; in other words, they furnish resistance to given power structures. Players involved in cultural studies and the dramatic arts question the world as is, as assumed to be not "naturally given," and generate change in all realms of daily, personal, and public life. Dramatic arts, in any form, from "low-brow" skits, school concerts, scripts, and popular culture, to "high-brow" productions and classical dramatic canons, are "packed" with constructions of cultural life that need to be "unpacked" to resist power relations.

Questions themselves are subject to interrogation. Who asks them? From what position of gender, race, class, sexuality, ethnicity, religion, politics, nationality, and personal and social history are the questions constructed? Whose questions and intentions are being privileged? By whom? Why? How? Caputo (1987) talks of "radical hermeneutics" in a manner conducive to critical cultural studies players—a questioner "is someone trying to make life difficult" (p. 189). Note that he says "difficult" not "impossible."

Lawrence Grossberg's definition in Probyn (1993) talks about cultural studies as concerned with describing and intervening in the ways discourses are produced within, and serve and operate in the relations between peoples' everyday lives and the structures of the social formation so as to reproduce, resist, and transform the existing structures of power (p. 2). Dramatic presentations subjected to the interrogations of power do not work in the abstract but are tied to everyday concrete descriptions of people, events, and settings.

At first, students in my dramatic arts classes seem anxious that they will not have examples of cultural constructions to present. They think that visibility, especially of gender, race, and physical differences, are the only area of study. Given only thirty seconds to select a scenario, they must spontaneously choose a cultural moment to present. One presentation was a classroom scene. A male teacher and two male and two female students comprised the scenario. The brief scenario was familiar. The teacher (a university student in role) was trying to teach a lesson while being distracted by two female students who kept putting up their hands (later it was argued that it is usually male students who try to attract the attention of the teacher). The interrogation began.

We asked who was in power? What was done, said, implied through body language that indicated power or powerlessness? What or who was valued? What and whose truths, knowledge, behavior were valued? What bureaucratic institutional power was portrayed? How? Why? How did it get to be this way? What signs, invisible and visible, demonstrated resistance to power? (Someone noticed the boys kept wanting to go to the bathroom, as a means of resisting the power of the teacher.) What historical constructions were in place? For example, we explored the historical influence of the church giving power to the one person at the front of the room and how this is played out in modern times. How were students represented? What truths or misrepresentations of teachers or students were there? How were each of us, as audience and cultural critics, positioned—for example, politically, historically, culturally, by gender, or race? Did that influence our dismantling? What cultural constructions were demonstrated in the class? Gender? yes; race? not visibly; sexual orientation? no; although in another mini-scenario, the heterosexual parents were challenged by the question: Why can't a family consist of two males or two females, in other words, homosexual, bisexual, or asexual?

The questioning continued. What became heated was the number of possible cultural constructions that could be questioned in many ways with many possible layers and plurality of meaning. What became evident to the students both as in-role and out-of-role participants were multiple possibilities for investigating and disrupting dramatic presentations. Also evident were the possible types of questions used to interrogate and dismantle the one-minute scenarios. Students learn the meaning of "cultural construction" and its possibilities, that is, as a phenomenon of human beings in social activity with historical influences that have carried on to the present day. Students were able to connect the points of Chapters 2 and 3, that is, with aspects of a modern cultural construction, what presents it, how it is presented, and how it is dismantled as problematic or in crisis.

The students learn that culture refers to many taken-for-granted and problematic webs of significance (Denzin, 1991, p. 73). Culture refers to any of the symbolic and significant meanings that humans produce; it is a medium that unites a range of different groups and communities in a common project with signifying systems by which groups, organizations, and institutions share an ideological force (Probyn, 1993, p. 119). Students realize that criticism is an investigation of the enabling conditions of the production of meaning in culture. What allows or creates these situations to emerge, circulate, and continue throughout modern times?

The exciting part for me about the students' awareness of cultural studies and criticism and its application to everyday life is their acceptance of both cultural studies and the dramatic arts as sites for the study of political struggle. Areas once taken for granted are brought to the foreground and challenged at very deep levels. Initially, some students mention they do not recognize the problematic issues that they see in context of the power play. Evident to the students and to myself is that sites of political struggle turn us into political "animals," so to speak, very aggressive in our interrogation of power. The one-minute scenarios through dramatic convention provide us with a safe site, allowing us an objective distance to portray someone other than ourselves; though in the long run, we realize that fantasy is borrowed from reality.

Both actors and audience can engage in the subject of inquiry whether it be knowledge, truth, cultural forms, differences, or exclusions. Whatever cultural form drama is, it is a safe environment. Cultural criticism represents a threat to existing dominance based on, for example, gender. Participants in the class are not able, when out of role, to distance themselves from the discussion. They become very defensive, especially the males, who, although dominated in numbers by the females, dominate when expressing their opinions and asking questions, an indication of the lack of value for women's knowledge and opinions.

The enabling conditions for the production of meaning in cultural constructions is somewhat limited. Students explore the surface of issues such as gender and race; although there are two or three races in the class, the European, white middle-class questions and dominance are still visible, in both the dramatic presentation and in the subsequent challenging. Difficult to determine are the factors that enable conditions of power and meaning to dominate others. The application of a historical aspect of hegemony becomes very difficult. Most thoughts and language have cultural stereotypes that influence interrogation. How do we dismantle self and our thinking? To objectively distance ourselves from the scenarios, yet be a part of it, whether our participation is in-role, in the audience, or in everyday life, creates heated discussions. A sense of humor, irony, and parody are very important to the seriousness of these interrogations. After a particular scenario was produced, I jokingly warned the students that they were not to bite each other, that once we left the room, we were to remain friends, that in this environment we are advocates of political struggle. As Leitch (1992) states: "[When] we become advocates of cultural studies, we are predisposed to intervene actively in issues of social struggle" (p. x). Concrete examples of cultural constructions available for interrogation and scrutiny are compacted objectively in dramatic moments.

DISCOURSE

Language is the major means by which subjects construct the world and are constructed by it. Language carries meaning; discourse carries power. Power is carried, yet left unchallenged, in language. One of the first theoretical venues to take the power in language seriously was the feminist movement in the 1960s and 1970s. Prior to that time, very few, if any, challenges were made to the "he" dominated world of knowledge. During my schooling in the 1950s and 1960s, even at university in the early 1970s, never was I made aware that the worlds of history, literature, sociology, psychology, and education were dominated by male truths, knowledge, writers, and speakers. Since then, gender-sensitive and -neutral language has shifted and balanced power, although the notions of exclusion go deeper than the use of "s/he." The feminist struggle resulted in policies that legislated inclusion. This is just one example of discourse created from resistance.

Foucault (1977) and Lyotard (1989) talk of language and power as discourse that produces and legitimizes the cultural logic of late capitalism. Witness the discourse of consumer advertising. It has saturated the lives of parents and children to the point where desire and need are blurred into the "I want—I need" generation of designer jeans and expensive running shoes. Hard work, saving money, and working for the goods are not part of the bourgeois nor the individual's discourse. Unfortunately, capitalist logic works from a position of privilege. Only those of that privileged class have the means to fulfill desires and needs. The discourse of capitalism excludes and seduces many into believing they desire, need, and are able to buy material goods.

The reader can take solace knowing that the "grand narrative" of cultural criticism in which this book is embedded is sometimes lost on my students (so they tell me); "the very people who live it, seek to [influence and inform but in the end] create their own elite discourse" (Agger, 1992, p. 25) that distances and excludes. Without esoteric discourse, the area of cultural criticism in the dramatic arts is not legitimized. I must admit to the crime of using grand narrative discourse. But as my mentor, Dorothy Heathcote, argues, I refuse to water down theory or any work in the dramatic arts.

Several theoretical principles of discourse are considered when rehearsing dramatic scenarios. A starting place is to have each student select a newspaper or news magazine story (avoid the personals, employment, and want ads) that contains an issue. For instance, the discourse around unwed mothers is especially powerful (I have yet to encounter the term "unwed fathers"). This discourse positions women as sinners, at fault, reminiscent of witch hunts. Somehow the discourse shifts to blame women—"the rise of teenage pregnancy," "the breakdown of the family unit," "the rise of sexual promiscuity," "the increase in prostitution" (a criminal offense) because of so many "young girls" on the street.

The discourse of news reporting presents the discourse of systems, images, and politics of power. "Unwed mother" discourse surrounds the article with many contexts that evoke discussion—for example, family, neighbors, the father's family, church, school, friends, hospital, government office, crisis line, news reporters, television anchor person, documentary writer, television show or soap opera. After a scenario, various discourses position young unmarried mothers' power. In whose words was power produced? How was power taken away from the subject? How do the politics of discourse play themselves out and inform the subjects, the policymakers, and others? The danger lies in the recycling of discourses that continue "to legitimize the practices that enable the existing set of representations to endure" (Zavarzadeh and Morton, 1994, p. 15). The enduring discourse surrounding young, unwed, pregnant women tropes them as "Salem Witches."

Other sites of power include the discourse surrounding "working-class" positions, unemployment, job creation and cutbacks, compensation, and welfare. Interestingly enough, the power remains in the agencies of government, industry, and big business. Rarely does it shift to the subjects, as agents of control or change. Although government agencies are "benevolent in intent, discourses and institutions that emerge with them often promote a deep and progressive disempowerment of their clients" (White, 1991, p. 8). Indeed, the discourse of welfare legitimizes and circulates the logic of capitalism. Media discourse of unemployment, job creation, and welfare positions and repositions people as dependent on capitalist rhetoric. Personal experiences of self, family, friends, and peers act as sites for power through discourse. This brings us to the point at which we will leave the grand narratives and focus on local and personal narratives as agencies for empowerment.

Grand narratives exclude small, local, and private narratives. The dramatic arts provide an excellent forum to value and rehearse the *petit recit*. The authenticity of "little" narratives working from the experiences, knowledge, values, and histories of private interests and needs encourages the reclaiming of "individual misfortunes and collectively representable grievances" (Benhabib, 1992, p. 9). Discourse generated by personal and local knowledge positions subjects differently. No longer silenced or excluded by grand narratives, the speaking subject (constituted by language) is in charge. Inquiry into what was formerly excluded, prohibited, or devalued suggests that "different questions can be asked and new and other voices can begin asking them" (Myrsiades and Myrsiades, 1994, p. 13). Voices of the oppressed, marginalized, abused, threatened, and the oppositional become empowered through the privilege and political power of the *petit recits.*

New paths of oppositional discourses intervene and resist dominant cultural constructions. One way, obviously, is to rewrite contemporary and classical scripts, to invent and insert discourse that changes the power, that moves the voices of the margins to the center. Another way, which works best in nonscripted, improvised works, is to stop the action of the play and have an audience member insert her/himself into the narrative in a manner that moves the discourse in a direction that empowers the powerless.

Habermas (1984) introduces several notions of language and power in a theory of communicative competence. A somewhat romantic and sometimes (dare I challenge an authority?) idealistic rendering of language, Habermas's "discourse ethics" tend to be exclusive of gender, race, and other issues of difference. During rehearsals or performances, participants seem more engaged when they accept the discourse and constructions as "natural" or "realistic." To challenge or interrupt the discourse is not acceptable. If intervention takes place (like meetings where men interrupt and women wait) merely to regain or keep power, then political action stays with certain groups or a dominant person. Discourse ethics is not simply looking at words or sentence structures but involves shifting the focus of language from the discursive (word level) to the figurative (the images created). In this way, discourse becomes a landscape of power systems and positions.

Language provides us with a major means of constructing and reconstructing our world. It provides the discourse necessary to stand outside and view the world, to reflect accordingly and then to reenter and take necessary actions to reconstruct the world. A Native American Lakota once told me that his culture had no equivalent to the white man's word "poverty." In his culture, poverty did not exist; he was not able to name it. When he used the word "poverty" as part of the Western Eurocentric discourse and stood back from his Native American culture, he realized that, by European discourse and definition, some Native Americans were indeed poor. Glance into Native American culture, decenter the Western Eurocentric discourse, and recognize not a lack of social order or poorer quality of life, but a criteria of what constitutes "poverty" imposed by a foreign culture.

In the postcritical, postmodern world, there is a necessary decline of discourse. Familiar linguistic constructs of grammar and vocabulary no longer serve the world. New discourse comes mainly from the poets, not just literary poets but political, economic, and social-cultural as well.

An excellent site for a poetic reconstruction of the social world is drama. Poets deconstruct old discourses to create new ideas and structures. The discourse in institutions, for example, was at one time exclusive, marginalizing groups and individuals. Special education, in its thrust to serve political agendas instead of interests, categorized individuals and groups as physically handicapped, mentally handicapped, retarded, crippled, dumb, learning disabled, gifted—a host of discriminatory categories. This discourse, on the one hand, was well intentioned; the purpose was to categorize for political funding. Labeling, however, ignored the fact that individual human needs have to be part of a larger sociocultural, political, and economic picture. In the labeling came the isolation. In this action of naming came the crime of powerlessness.

Discourse that names is problematic when people begin to construct the world accordingly. When the discourse changes to, for example, "physically challenged," we recognize a special difference based on physical needs that are different from physically unchallenged people. In the past, special discourses isolated and denied access to certain people who fit the label. The postcritical world would accommodate and mainstream all people. Discourse that includes humans as part of a social order does not oppress, marginalize, or devalue. Drama's playfulness of words and rehearsal of discourses provides an arena for reconstructing discourse that is inclusive and necessary to embody the discourse, the critical consciousness, and reveal the existing discourses of domination and control. Participants begin a reconstruction of the social field of human thought and behavior.

The discourse of the early environmental movement supplied a language that voiced the problems of mass industrialization and population growth. Problems—air, water, and soil pollution, industrial waste, deforestation, and chemical spills—initiated action.

In North America, there is an increasing number of homeless people. The discourse, as it now exists, tends to put the homeless people in a position of blame. The homeless have been rendered politically, economically, and socially powerless, in large part, by a discourse of dependency on welfare and outdated social support systems. Discourse about homelessness as a result of the failure of the domination of capitalization, when people can no longer contribute to the capitalist society, when consumerism is controlled by national and multinational corporations, and when individuals no longer fit the production mode, shifts positions, blame, and power from the centers to the margins—where the homeless live. Even their homes become marginalized; they live on the fringes of urban centers or in areas next to the wealth of urban blight. In Toronto, for example, at the Pantages Theatre, where people pay from forty to a hundred dollars to see *The Phantom of the Opera,* or go around the corner to see *Les Miserables* (the very play that talks about the rise of nationalism and exclusion), we find a population of at least ten thousand homeless people.

Dramatic artists, informed by cultural criticism, ask: How do we talk about this? How do we present/perform this condition? How do we shift the responsibility of political and institutional power for this condition? How do we relocate the homeless into a position of agency? What discourse moves them to challenge and resistance? How do we provide a discourse that sees this situation as problematic so we can begin the process of transformation? Sometimes people who should have access to cultural and artistic constructs of society are the very people for whom access is denied.

Social action theater, some types of community theater, and political theater already make critical questions part of their mandate. Boal (1985), a Brazilian, well known for Theater of the Oppressed, bases his work on a Marxist perspective. In North America, some of his fundamental principles hold sway, but the contexts in which he works are different. What North Americans perhaps do not see is that besides being oppressors of South American countries, there is mass oppression within their own countries. How American wealth and domination are dependent on colonization of South American economic and political systems would be threatening to the status quo—if not impossible in a bourgeois-dominated system. Resistance to the oppression of North Americans becomes distorted. Recognition requires openness to the discourse, and acceptance of the constructs for resistance, to become sincere and authentic. If I invite abused women, homeless persons, or street kids into drama classes, resistance comes from the academic institution to nonacademic persons. Yet these very people, who should have access to the discourse and structures of oppression, can provide academics with insights necessary for a true remodeling of social inequities and a source of action. The claim that our social programs are being cut back distracts us from the issue. The discourse of economic cutbacks should serve to reconstruct the social imagination. Drama can be a safe, experimental haven for reimagining the social world.

Take, for instance, a drama on homelessness. We could reenact the conditions; it makes for sensationalism and most likely would sell at the box office. Cultural studies theater would then ask different questions of the situation. Who gets to be homeless? How? Critical questions make us enter the world of homelessness at a different point than does "reality"; we enter at the point of deconstruction where we take apart the reason for the increase in homelessness instead of examining the reality of how it feels. The dominance of reality-based theater departs from the throes of natural representation and depiction and into "the making of" (the construction of) homelessness. Social action theater, informed by social vision theater, ideally provides insights and strategies that empower individuals and social groups to construct a quality of world that is inclusive.

POWER

The most contentious thread of modern life is systems of power in any cultural constructions that create situations, moments, subjects, histories, and practices of exclusions, exclusions based on differences from the status quo, the standard, the norm, the right, the traditional, the accepted, the fashionable, the absolute, or the singular. In a roundabout way, this is almost the claim of modern life—that every aspect of the world is in a state of power that forces questions such as: Whose and what power is dominant? How did it get to be so? What does the placement of power do to exclude other worlds, other knowledges, other ways of being, or ways of structuring the world that are inclusive? How can the systems or constructions of power be questioned to reveal and transform dominations and exclusions?

As a vehicle for the application of cultural studies, both scripted and nonscripted dramatic arts agitate the power dimensions of representations sometimes neutralized by the surface or entertainment aspect of drama. Students' reluctance and nervousness in Cultural Studies through Theater classes are especially evident in rehearsals or performances where opinions, thoughts, choices, and biases are public. One way students "go public" comfortably is through warm-up games where students present raw versions of a scenario, and subject the scenario to questions about power and authority, questions of truth, representation, and how institutional structures support domination and ascribe meanings. The rehearsal process is as important for the questioning of power as it is for representation and recognition of power.

The rise or challenge of any cultural construction is, according to Wiseman (1989), usually determined by material interest. The interests of the dominant social class, regardless of political leanings, are reflected in the knowledge produced and the codes and conventions that conform to the establishment. A drive for power through money excludes the collective aspects of human existence and, instead, makes individuals competitive. Production of unequal power relations result in privilege and power at the center and dependent individuals on the margins. This is the hegemonic project of the middle class in operation. Dismantling these obvious dramatic scenes or situations of power in everyday life becomes elusive. The dominance and comfort of "middle ground" perspectives makes surveying cultural landscape for examples of power not easy for the neutral, already privileged, or uninformed participant. Dismantling systems of power, even those presented by the fictional world of drama, might reflect the interests of the dominant more so than unpack entrenched power constructions.

Students, informed by cultural studies theories, were asked to investigate fairytales. Several attempts did redistribute and, in one case, balance power relations based on gender, race, class, institutions (family, kingdoms), and physical and intellectual differences. Both the participants and the audience, however, found it difficult to eliminate dominant power structures. Reconstructing became more a "shifting" of power or role reversal—man for woman roles, middle class or poor for wealthy, wheelchair-bound for non-wheelchair-bound. What was unavailable were concrete examples of alternative tropes or modes of construction that truly dismantled and created a space where "cultural knowledge is in the service of the subject, [where] the goal is not the legitimization of power but the enabling of empowerment" (Benhabib, 1992, p. 205).

Empowerment is a precarious world to rehearse. Besides the danger of frivolity in presenting scenes of power and oppression for real-world interrogation is the possible suppression or annihilation of relationships, structures, images, knowledge, or values. Offers of new cultural constructions can be silenced by the exclusion of any form and possibility of empowerment. The burden of cultural studies is to rehearse realities of inclusion not assimilation, to negotiate between the multiplicity of all possible cultural constructions and forms of empowerment (where subjects have a sense of agency and efficacy), and "produce knowledges that are aware of their political constitution" (Zavarzadeh and Morton, 1994, p. 136).

One of the dominant forces in the construction of our world has been the Hollywood film. The texts and the actors have produced a worldwide acceptance of Hollywood constructs as an authority on how the world should or could be. The colonization of our lives and, one could argue, the colonization of our minds are powerful influences in contemporary culture. Power given to a Tom Hanks, Tom Cruise, Julia Roberts, and others gives an implicit authority to a film's content and structure and to the construction of knowledge, values, and beliefs created and legitimized by Hollywood. In other words, their actions and words become integrated as ways of thinking about and ways of being in our world. Dangerously so.

Actors remain bigger than life on a movie screen or matrixes on a smaller screen, and they are without challenge from the viewers. Viewers might criticize the actors' portrayals or even their acting abilities, yet disregard the movie's implications for real life. In one way, this is very McLuhanian, in that the medium is the message or Baudrillard's hyper-reality or simulacra. Without the application of cultural criticism theory, drama of this type becomes assumptive and without challenge to the authority of the text.

Of course, true liberation and transformation comes only through our realization of these theories in our everyday lives. Quasi-courageous is the person who writes about oppression, resistance, liberation, and transformation. Courageous is the person who stands forth in the everyday, recognizes oppression, and offers resistance and transformation. Whether as an individual, or as part of a group, the responsibility is to guide ourselves and others toward a reconstruction of our world. The means by which we do this does not necessarily justify the end. Fundamentalism, neoconservatism, violence in words and deeds, force of any kind, evangelical promises, and preaching do not work. It has been traditionally within the great discourses, the grand narratives as Lyotard (1989) states, that social action has happened. The great religious narratives of Buddhism, Judaism, Christianity, Islam, and others have transformed the social structures of the world, as have the theories of thinkers like Marx and Mills. Quietly moving throughout history, women have changed the world. Drama can act as a dominant means to interrogate and restructure our world. It can be peaceful or revolutionary, violent or quiet; however, it can and should be purely a time and space in which people gather together as spectators and participants to rehearse resistance and reconstructions.

Any area of curriculum is open to examination by the ideologies and practices of cultural studies, including the latter's own assumptions. The discussion introduced so far obviously favors the dramatic arts as a major, creative, and safe means of operating within the framework of cultural studies. At this point, it is necessary to hear other voices within cultural studies that are borrowed from critical/postcritical theory and modernism/postmodernism so that we can explore the implications for drama in education.

CHALLENGE AND RESISTANCE

The "work" of the arts and cultural studies is to reveal and identify "power" as it exists in the everyday. Without tension, without resistance or challenge to the familiar, to the taken-for-granted, the arts and cultural studies are mere pretensions. Power is revealed through the painter's brush, the playwright's words, the dancer's body, and the cultural critic's questions. Cultural studies, like the dramatic arts, is committed to producing tension—to reveal and to resist. Power is the mainstay of nature (a beautiful scene can take our breath away), art (Mona Lisa's smile has entranced for centuries), and drama (Hamlet has been played somewhere at least once every year since it was written). This is the power that is awesome, that elevates us, that challenges us to wonder, to think deeply.

Power in cultural studies is political. Power privileges, suppresses, silences, marginalizes, imprisons, and destroys. Power isolates and eliminates differences—differences in values, truths, knowledge, and histories, differences based on gender, race, age, and other cultural constructions. To gain power for differences, we turn to politics. As cultural critics, our first actions should be to challenge and resist dominant powers. In real life, however, there is often limited to nil action. Power remains unchallenged for a variety of reasons and to avoid unpleasant consequences. We accept the status quo as the norm.

Power exists in many forms and degrees. The first step to challenging it is to recognize it. Through any of the dramatic arts, everyday life can be economized, simplified, slowed down, or stilled. Application of cultural studies questions and theories position the participants for the investigation of power present in the presentations, and for the rehearsal of potential strategies of resistance.

Power and resistance also are cultural constructs, an important theoretical point to restate. Once questions of power are asked (see earlier in this chapter and Chapter 6 for examples of foregrounding the question), resistance and challenge struggle to dismantle the dominant power of certain truths over others. A belief in this principle is vital to dramatic arts rehearsals and presentations. Dominant ideologies and systems of power continue to be created, circulated, and reproduced. Acceptance of the fact that power and resistance are culturally constructed demands that we ask "what other factors were necessary for the arrival [of power], for getting and staying there?" (Probyn, 1993, p. 71).

In one class scenario, several power systems exposed themselves. The setting was a living room/kitchen area. Father/husband and son were watching a football game with a male friend while mother/wife was ironing in the kitchen. The stereotypes abounded. Father (burping beer) and son engaged in armchair cheering and commentating (including cheerleader comments that would make the television character Al Bundy proud). The power structures were easy to investigate: female passiveness and domestication, domination of male sports, control of programming, master/slave relationships (son implicitly learning a cultural construction from his father). The actors worked with status quo notions. No one asked: What sustained the power? How did it get to be that way? Why does it stay that way? When audience members were asked to intervene physically, in other words, to change or balance the power structures by walking into the scenario, hints of resistance surfaced. Some were subtle, some verged on violence. Where role shifting occurred, the "new" mother challenged the request to "Get me another beer, honey" by dumping the beer on her husband's head—an act that would lead to another act of violence. The offered selections of resistance were limited in large part, I assume, by a lack of understanding of what resistance is and of how one resists, that is, the limited constructions of resistance, other than violence, in our collective imaginations.

Resistance to power and authority (expertise) is the most significant yet difficult element to produce. We need to direct ourselves. Political and cultural workers are directed to action, and they change especially that which is most directly related to everyday, taken-for-granted lives. What are we to resist? Power, yes, but as an abstract term, how does resistance to power play out in the everyday? Identification of the many forms and levels of power is another problem with resistance, as discussed before, as is the limited repertoire of appropriate resistance formats. The most difficult aspect to overcome when applying resistance theories and practices is the existence of hegemony (elaborated further in Chapter 5).

"Hegemony" is a term used by Gramsci (1973) to refer to unchallenged, unquestioned systems and practices of power. Gramsci's imprisonment, due to his resistance to the Fascist regime of Italy, led him to analyze power and extend the notion of hegemony. He asked why, who, and what constituted systems of power that allowed it to be produced, circulated, and sustained without question. Capitalist systems of the West function seductively to make resistance unnecessary or, at least, unnatural. The bourgeois class system remains intact. Complacency, neutrality, and conformity are dominant while images of wealth, health, freedom, and democracy are circulated as commodities accessible to "all" Westerners. So what is there to resist, why and how? If we are masters, experts, or victims of hegemony (it surrounds and comforts us), is there really any reason to resist? Perhaps an unpacking of a typical day would reveal not only power and dominance but examples of hegemony.

A stage. Three couples are asleep in their beds—a young man and woman, a middle-aged man and woman, and an elderly man and woman. The alarm rings and the day begins for each one. Each character is given a different persona: race, sexuality, physical and mental differences, history, career, immigrant status—whatever differences constitute subjects and determine, in large measure, their daily encounters with power, resistance, authority, and hegemony. Questions about power are asked. Who gets to wake up when? Why? How did it get to be that way? What differences have isolated, oppressed, excluded this person from mainstream local life? What institutional systems are already present—explicitly and implicitly (e.g., furniture design, space; for instance, does the wife sleep on the side of the bed next to the alarm clock?). How is the everyday routine constructed by power that remains unquestioned, unchallenged? Are there any small or large acts of resistance? Why or why not? What hegemonic practices were displayed, circulated, accepted, obvious, not obvious? Each person's walk through a tunnel of daily scenarios would bring forth a multitude of possible examples to freeze for scrutiny and reflection. How are our days, weeks, months, years, lives arranged by family, church, school, community, friends, popular culture, media, history, books, local or international representations that produce and protect power and the powerful?

Resistances need articulation; that is, exactly what is the shape of the power that needs to be resisted? Resistance needs a shape so as not to move as invisible acts among the ghosts of power. Some forms of power that resistance addresses are: theories and practices that totalize, bureaucracy, establishment, representations, systems, meanings, truths, records, texts, literatures, contradictions, categories, labels, discourses, knowledge, authority, expertise, symbolic representations, grand narratives, stories of other, of self, ideologies, military right, news reports, magazines, commodified desires, borders, policies, legislations, government, conformity, and, in summary, "modern life."

We might suffer from exhaustion but the arts provoke and use time, space, body, and action to rehearse resistance with an economy of meaning, rigor, and safety. A multiplicity of cultural constructions forces into the open the falsehood of power, the hegemonic consensus of what seems natural, normal, or common sense. Theories and practices that celebrate resistance and cultural criticism in the "real" world will be explored in more depth under the principles of hegemony and counter-hegemony (see Chapter 7).

POPULAR CULTURE

One cannot talk about cultural studies and the dramatic arts without discussing popular culture and its technologies. The invasion of mass media, music, television, film, videos, and personal computers has saturated our daily and international lives. They have become the major constructors of knowledge, values, history, institutions, power, and positioning of subjects. Where, at one time, people quoted the law, classics, experts, church, and academics, they now quote the Anita Hill or O.J. Simpson trials, Jerry Seinfeld, *ER,* situation comedies, soap operas and, of course, *Oprah*! Expertise, personal testimonies, and a great variety of cultural constructions are available to the masses especially with the globalization (and homogenization) of culture through the media. Even when American celebrities fall from grace, they are still, or become even more, commodifiable.

The privilege given to content and forms of popular culture is important to cultural criticism and the dramatic arts for reasons discussed previously. Whose truths, knowledge, stories are privileged? Who is represented? Misrepresented? How? How is culture constructed by the medium? How are subjectivities constructed? Ad infinitum. The bombardment of popular cultural constructions impacts on the consciousness; they erase the boundaries between the private and the public celebrity culture. They set up epistemological logic in a world (living rooms and lounges) where resistance and challenges are unspoken or unheard, where differences are eradicated by politically neutral content and forms, where subjectivity is constructed by constant proliferating representations over which the audience has no control or space to challenge. This leaves mass media and culture, without the scrutiny of dismantling theories, in crisis. Dramatic arts depictions, borrowed from mass media culture, allow for a selection of significant content, for reflection and questioning on slowed-down and freeze-framed action, and finally, for rethinking and reconstructing cultural representations.

To accept the power of popular culture representations means accepting cultural productions of the margins, that is, practicing hegemony. Although popular culture does expose injustices, a large portion of the works, whether in tabloids, news journals, film, or computer programs, goes unchallenged. Furthermore, political action by a few becomes censorship instead of open dialogue with the mass audience who become "a public turned into victims of a homogenized [and unchallenged] mass culture" (Denzin, 1991, p. 3). Crossing between the genres and strategies of popular culture and dramatic arts opens doors for multiple readings, resistance, and the establishment of counter-hegemonic practices.

The major crisis in popular culture is the decline and commodification of public discourse. Discourse becomes threatened by double-edged words and catch-22's. Multiple representations, stories, and voices are produced through multiple discourses; however, these discourses are reduced to thirty-second bites and seven-minute clips. The power to structure discourse and the consciousness of mass media consumers lie in the hands of a few. These few behind-the-scenes people construct, select, and circulate established cultural systems—bourgeois in popularity, and apolitical in content and consumer agency (other than turning it off or throwing it out).

Over the years, I have seen an increase in the influence of popular culture on the play and learning of kindergarten to university students. They (and I) copy representations, quote television and film stars as experts and, in the dramatic arts (my major area of teaching), often borrow images, content, and forms from the media. They borrow without scrutiny, without challenge, and without awareness of power and exclusions. The contradictions, to them, are invisible, normal, and natural. Statements like "That's the way it's supposed to be" and "Life's like that" legitimize the media to select, construct, and circulate subjectivities and actions, and their only challenge comes from advertisers and the Nielsen ratings. The gift of "live" drama and the texture of humans present to each other in rehearsals are examples of Habermas's discourse ethics and cultural studies as political acts.

POSITIONING

What do cultural studies theories and practices imply for the investigation and disruption of cultural constructions using the dramatic arts? One way to produce flexible, yet rigorous, rehearsal sessions is to direct from the notion of positioning. Positioning refers to the placement of subjects (not characters) in relation to others' truths and knowledge. How do these representations position the subject (in-role) in terms of power, authority, oppression, silence, exclusion, inclusion, privilege, or disadvantage? In other words, how are the subjects positioned (in-role) that prevent or allow them political action for resisting power that excludes differences?

To clarify positioning as a political act, I will relate some examples from everyday life and from what has emerged during rehearsal processes. We are all positioned in time, space, body, and in relation to others. Cultural studies "looks at how various cultural forms [truths, knowledge, history, gender, age, etc.] 'position' the subject" (Lash, 1989, p. 19). As we work with the questions and theories of cultural studies, the major focus is: How does the subjects' positioning affect (increase, limit, prevent) their empowerment? agency? Such a focus yields the following kinds of questions: How can subjects resist their positions? Who blocks their challenge? How? What are the contradictions between subjects' positions of power or powerlessness? What cultural forms or histories are advancing or blocking the subjects' positioning? How is positioning of power based on differences (gender, age, etc.)? What maintains positions (history, popular culture, discourse, traditions, texts, arts, sciences)? How? How are subjects positioned by categories, titles, birth, borders, religion, education? The possibilities of positioning are limitless for observing, resisting, and changing power systems. The rehearsal sessions in which to do this may be limited. The collective imagination is not.

Whereas the arts traditionally functioned from the premise of universality, that is, from the individual (truth, history, etc.) to the collective (solidarity is necessary), cultural studies questions universality because it excludes differentiated culture forms and people (Miller, 1990, p. 172). Examples abound in terms of positioning as a political act. Said observes that "the Orient is there to enable the Occident, Africa is there to enable western civilization to fulfil its mission, the woman is there to help men actualize himself in her womb" (in Benhabib, 1992, p. 15). Positioning—victim/rapist, master/slave, landowner/peasant, director/actor, husband/wife, boss/staff, young/old, adult/child, teacher/student, heterosexual/homosexual/bisexual, writer/reader. Why is this so? Could it be that hegemonic practices create and maintain certain subject positioning as natural, historical, and right?

These paragraphs about positioning provide information to be used during rehearsal processes. The ideas expressed provoke participants and audience to action—actions that observe, resist, and change the positioning of subjects, truths, and so forth in a world of power and oppression, privilege, and dependence, voice, and silence. The dramatic arts are used to fracture the cultural constructions of the status quo. Cultural studies gives priority to alternative subject positioning (see Toni Morrison, 1992, for the repositioning of the master/slave tradition in the white imagination). Dramatic arts open rehearsals and presentations to a variety of possible subject positions. From our position in cultural studies and the dramatic arts, we must ask how and why we speak for others. And, really, can we truly speak for the "other"? We position ourselves as theorists and artists "who are able to occupy numerous, different, sometimes apparently conflicting positions on a continuum of cultural categories and discourses" (Auslander, 1992, p. 53).

CHAPTER 4

Deconstruction of Cultural Constructions

INTRODUCTION

Chapters 1, 2, and 3 were intended to provide a history and a context from whence cometh contemporary theories of cultural criticism. Some dramatic practices are included in those chapters, but serve mainly to present dramatic scenarios taken from everyday contexts and content. Once presented, these scenarios become texts open to interrogations that dismantle cultural constructions of dominance, power, privilege, marginalization, oppression, exclusion, silence, and invisibility. As discussed in Chapter 3, the major means of interrogation is the question. Questions driven by cultural studies are already a challenge; they initiate the dismantling of modern constructions of truth, knowledge, history, institutions, popular culture, language, and subjectivity. Once informed, questions, whether private or public, can find an even safer and more creative site through dramatic play and strategies.

It is important to discuss again the definition of culture. Culture is shared symbols, signs, rituals, and behaviors, and assumes that meanings are socially produced. An individual may create the text but does so in a social and historical context. Culture, in critical theory and postmodern discourse, refers to any context in which meanings are generated, especially through symbolic representations. Culture can therefore refer to a set of meanings based on gender, race, color, creed, sexuality, political affiliations, and other possible constructions.

The major tenets of cultural studies serve as theoretical tools used to investigate and dismantle texts. One of these theories is deconstruction.

When most people hear the word "text," they tend to think of print. Text, however, is any group of meanings that are visual, audio, musical, literature, advertisement, and so forth. Text is full of signs and symbols that generate meaning and, in this way, are embedded with cultural constructions. The project of deconstruction is to look at the generated truths, knowledge, history, representations, and uncover the positions, exclusions, misrepresentations, and dominance.

Modern texts are the dominant construction; they are, in fact, the prevalent force driving Western countries. The truths and knowledge that we possess today derive mostly (if not all) from the "modern" constructions of truth, that is, "Western"—developed from European, Mediterranean, and, more recently, American history with roots in Hebrew, Latin, and Greek. Immersed in modern crisis, texts of positioning are deconstructed from Western contexts. It is the dominant site in which we are located and from which we work.

Different from deconstruction and dismantling text is critical analysis. Several assumptions in analysis have traditionally been considered in, especially, printed text. Two major assumptions were that meaning is fixed, and mainly is generated through language. Someone said, "This is the truth"; "This is how it is." Historically, the Hebrew people regarded Moses and his tablets as the truth. Jesus Christ subsequently challenged the Hebrew texts, truths, and cultural constructions. He presented different truths—a new construction of reality from which arose institutions and bureaucracies to legitimize and support this new truth, Christianity, that is, Catholicism and "Protest"antism. More recently in Christian churches, for example, there are cries of exclusion from this original truth. One need only look at the separation between the Protestant and Catholic churches to wonder how this happened. Was it because certain people or values were excluded from the doctrine or did not have any power? Challenges, interrogations, and dismantlings lead to change and political action. What accumulates is a history of resistance to credos and the grand narratives that are totalizing but not inclusive and also structure culture in such a manner that privileges and assigns power.

Analysis in the past, whether literary, political, critical, or otherwise, worked on the principle of fixed truths, knowledge, values, history, and other cultural artifacts. At some point, exclusions and positions were noted; that is, it was recognized that people have different experiences and work from different positions in time, space, and gender. Differences change meanings, resulting in multiple meanings or possibilities of constructions, beginnings, middles, and endings, privileging of differences, plurality, and nonclosure, or no conclusions (which is very unlike the empirical methods and desired closure of the modern consciousness of rationality). This multiplicity of meanings provides the ecstasy that Barthes (1986) refers to as the "joissance" in the deconstruction of texts.

THREE TYPES OF TEXT READINGS

Before I connect the oppositional reading of cultural texts required to deconstruct modern life, two other traditional types of readings will be discussed. The first is a dominant or "preferred" reading. The reader accepts, without question or challenge, the dominant constructions that are found in the text. Traditionally, school and the way we have been taught to read has produced "preferred readers." In school, there is usually only one fixed response. Agreement is with the dominant discourse. Someone has made the decision that it is the right one. The answer represents absolute truth and fixed knowledge. There is no questioning of the representations of culture.

The second kind of reading (for the purpose of cultural studies) is "negotiated." In a negotiated reading, readers accept some of the generated meanings and reject others. For example, in the text of the O.J. Simpson trial, a preferred reading sounds like, "It was a fair trial; I accept the verdict." A negotiated reading claims, "Yes, it was a fair trial, but I do not accept that the police messed up the evidence" or "I do not accept the part where Furhman changed the trial." Negotiated readings mediate between the truths of the text and those of the reader. The third kind of reading is oppositional or resistant. In action, resistance and challenge in deconstruction is constant, and based mainly on the politics of difference. Oppositional readings position the text of the O.J. Simpson trial from the point of view of race, gender, and other cultural constructions; examine the dominant, privileged, powerless, and devalued constructions, challenge them, and produce multiple readings, that is, oppositional readings of gender, race, age, media, class, and mythology. For example, O.J. Simpson was regarded as a sports hero; he is now another kind of hero, but, for different races, that heroism has been redefined. Are there any other ways that we could read the O.J. text? Gates (1995) in *The New Yorker* writes about "Thirteen Ways of Looking at a Black Man," placing the public readings of the O.J. trial under the scrutiny of thirteen black cultural leaders. Additional readings, laid out for public display through the media, challenged the notion of the "expertise" of lawyers, judges, and DNA experts. The experts were challenged;

loopholes were found in their knowledge and truths, and the deconstruction continues.

Barthes (1986), a French philosopher whom some would call a poststructuralist, uses organic and sexual discourse to talk about the act of reading a text. He speaks of most readings as *plaissir* (pleasure), of being a "readerly" text (of any text, printed, oral, and so on). He compares this with the kind of reader who reads text in a state of *joissance,* who finds ecstasy in challenge, in the urge to deconstruct text and resist dominant cultural constructions by reading "against the grain." This kind of reader refuses to negotiate the constructions of modern life, especially those that are not truthful from the reader's position. Reading "with the grain" or a dominant reading is seen as an act of control, power, and exclusion based on difference.

Reading a text means that text can be anything that is socially constructed. Of the three kinds of readings previously described, we assume that cultural studies includes the latter two types, especially oppositional readings. Fixed meanings and the way we read texts are decontextualized; that is, we read texts as if they are in and of themselves. In cultural studies, every text is written and read from within a context—historical, economical, gender, race, and so forth. An oppositional reading, that is, reading against the grain does not makes claims of "Aha! That is the quintessential article or book on that text." Rather, we deconstruct the text, oppose and negotiate multiple readings, beginnings, endings—a polyphony of interpretations.

For those of us in the school system, there are many implications. One of the crises in education is that we standardize; we like things the same, so there has to be fixed meanings to control and test. A text has several possible meanings depending on the position of the reader or the writer in time, space, and from the constructed sites of gender, race, class, age, and so forth. For example, when a journal article has the theme "evaluation," the article is read or written from a dominant or preferred position. When I write articles for journals, I read several copies of the journal because I can tell by the included articles just what kind of writings the editors "prefer" (What type of writings do they want to get? What kind of readings?). I do not usually submit a writing that challenges mainstream, dominant text constructions because the editor or audience would not necessarily want that article to be published (subscription value, perhaps?). From a cultural studies' point of view, articles are written in opposition to one another to provide multiple readings of a text or author. For example, in a recent volume of the journal

Cultural Studies (1995), each article discusses the works of Toni Morrison from a different position; in this way, deconstructing the text while presenting decentered (from mainstream Eurocentric) multiple readings and realities of Afro-Americans.

DECONSTRUCTION

The major exponent of deconstruction theory is Derrida. His theory, however, in the context of the dramatic arts, remains elusive, esoteric, and downright obscure (which he revels in). Although several features mark the boundaries of Derrida's work, the primary concept to grasp is "the instability of language" (Sarup, 1993, p. 32). This implies that the means and ends of using language can never be immediately clear nor understood as a one-to-one association. The signs, which in dramatic representations are given through voice, space, time, movement, body, otherness, and silence, can be identical in different contexts. However, the meanings of these signs can vary from context to context and through the spatial and temporal processes of language use. If we combine this with Heidegger's (1977) notion of language "being the house in which we dwell," the instability of language also refers to the instability of who we are. Thus interpretations and human existence are never a stable or fixed entity. The procedure that Derrida applies to text is called deconstruction, where texts are used "reflexively to unsettle and shatter the original distinctions" (Sarup, 1993, p. 35).

Through the rehearsal process of using actor, voice, text, body, gestures and a host of other theatrical strategies, the dramatic arts contribute naturally to Derrida's notions of deconstruction of textual meanings and criticism. Since the play of drama never ends, the search for pure or final expression never occurs. For example, the play *Hamlet* has been acted and re-acted through a multiplicity of historical, political, and social contexts, each one deriving its meaning from our "present perceptual world as we are experiencing it" (Sarup, 1993, p. 35).

Another major concept of deconstructionsm as espoused by Derrida is the notion of language as logocentric and phonocentric. In the past, speech was given priority over writing. Meaning was associated with the immediacy of presence, especially apparent when using the inner voice of consciousness. In logocentrism, the word was given final consciousness and without the mediation of presence or internal meaning. When we speak the words of a text through dramatic modes, spoken words seem to come from a real being. On the other hand, writing is indirect and removed from the "silent conversation of consciousness" (Sarup, 1993, p. 36). Derrida challenges this privileging of voice as a medium of meaning. In the dramatic arts, however, the logos of the text is deconstructed through the phonocentrism of voice and actor. His points are well taken and have implications for the dramatic arts as a means of interpretation and understanding of text.

When we listen to the voices of drama taken from the text, we cannot assume that what is being spoken is meaningful or truthful. Dramatic arts should be seen rather as a conversation or dialogue, as a mediator between text and audience. The actor with the skill in this area is the one who can deconstruct and move the logocentric world of text to the phonocentric meaning of the words spoken. The implications of Derrida's notion of deconstruction for the dramatic arts offers a theoretical foundation for other culturally constructed texts.

Another feature of Derrida's deconstruction is the politics of metaphor. Metaphor means that a word is not taken at its face value nor can it be given a fixed meaning. There must be a link between the phonocentrism and logocentrism of speech, and of printed text. In addition there is the Heiddeggerian or phenomenological notion that all words are metaphorical. Reflexivity turns the text not back on ourselves, but back on itself in terms of a metaphorical stance. This again supports the notion of the instability of language because we could argue that the sign and the signifier are always in a metaphorical flux, a task that drama has been laden with for centuries.

To look, in concrete terms, at constructs through language, we can name a table as such because in the literal sense we see the table as a table. When we look at the metaphorical sense of "table" we see "table" used in many contexts with many meanings. We can "table" a set of figures. We can "table" or hold back a set of motions in a parliamentary procedure until the next meeting. If we "table" something or lay it out on a flat surface, we look at it quite differently. In other words, "table" becomes connected to new concepts or actions, and serves as a possibility to create new knowledge, images, and texts.

We can always argue for a metaphor so that the naming of the word becomes the issue and metaphorical politics does not move us into rhetorical argument. In the undoing of opposites, as we give attention to metaphor, we realize that language simply does not just reflect reality but helps to constitute it. In order to reconstruct our world, the responsibility is to reissue and rework our metaphors. As Sarup (1993) writes, "There are no final conclusions; the text can never be fixed and as a result it can never be deciphered either" (p. 45).

In *Tropics of Discourse,* White (1978) states language can become a prison but the application of critical discourse can deconstruct the metaphorical world. This impulse should drive the dramatic arts to deconstruct culturally constructed texts, to thereby release us from believing that language and thus text are to be taken literally.

Metaphors are about relationships. In our postmodern world, relationships to self and others are in a stage of reconstruction. Through the dramatic arts and with the application of deconstruction theories and method (such as erasure and metaphor), a reading that privileges the reader and decenters the text is a movement toward the liberation of text from the prison of fixed meanings. Deconstruction without the consideration of sociocultural, political, and historical implications can be violent and extreme in the reconstruction or restructuring of social imaginations. To replace the old ways with the entirely new is not necessarily the duty of deconstructionism.

MULTIPLICITY AND NONCLOSURE

When we watch a film or television, read a book, or observe a text, at the same time that we look for questions, exclusions, dominance, power, and meaning, we come to recognize the potential for multiple readings. If we apply deconstruction theories and methods, if we read the text from positions of difference such as race, class, history, or truth, multiple readings are the outcome. If, in the dramatic arts, we go in-role and position actors and audience (in-role) differently as, for example, mothers, daughters, grandmothers, how would the text be read based on the different constructions of gender, history, age, class, mythology, sexuality, and so forth? Dependent on our in-role position and while maintaining dramatic dignity and honor to the role, how would we deconstruct the text? What would be presented as power? As dominance? As privilege? How would the text be read if a homosexual reader sought the contradictions and exclusions in the text? We would see power quite differently. We would challenge representations because they are false, distorted, or even invisible. Not only do we get multiple meanings but we propagate multiple beginnings, middles, and endings—multiple structures, multiple discourses.

One of the crises in modern life is the consuming desire for theoretical and practical activities to reach consensus and closure. If not, we feel incomplete or extremely disconcerted when there is not a recognizable end, a completion of thought, action, word, or structure based on the familiar. When we read a book or watch a film, we need familiar structures with which to relate. We need to leave the film or finish the book knowing that an ending is in place. We like structures with recognizable sequences. These are modern constructions of texts and of our lives. When we question and deconstruct these structures, we have more than one way to begin, to end, to apply meaning. Fairytales, for example, "once upon a time" and "they lived happily ever after," are modern texts, relied upon for their familiar structures, meanings, beginnings, and endings. How do we really remain true to these textual constructions and true to the multiple realities, truths, experiences of different lives?

Postmodern fairytales that recognize the differences of gender, race, age, and so forth in our culture, deconstruct the dominant white, European, male texts of our culture. Deconstruction of fairytales, for instance, says that construction is taken for granted, that it is not natural, it excludes, there is dominance. If we read the text (fairytales, for instance) from different positions (e.g., gender, race), then we will get different beginnings, middles, and ends, and definitely multiple readings.

In *Pulp Fiction* (1994), for example, we leave the movie with no clear idea of beginning, middle, or end in terms of familiar structure, narrative, content, or purpose. When the "beginning" occurs we accept it as the beginning—chronologically and familiarly. Beginnings and endings can be chronological, but if we refer theoretically or philosophically, there may be various beginnings and endings throughout any story. In *Pulp Fiction,* the end of the film could be the beginning or the middle. Upon reflection, there are many possible places that could be the beginning, middle, or ending of the movie. These possibilities change with each rereading or reviewing of the text. This constant dismantling or deconstruction of the text makes us, as one student so aptly put it, "think and rethink how we take things like violence for granted."

There are different kinds of deconstructionism just as there are different kinds of existentialism (Marxist, feminist, or Sartre's existentialism). There is no fixed meaning or definition in deconstructionist philosophy. If we accept Sartre's truth as absolute, then we would never have different theories of existentialism. Fixed meanings mean fixed worlds, worlds that exclude, privilege, and marginalize, and that silence truths, knowledge, histories, and other elements of power. The discourse of any one view tends to totalize, to become a "grand narrative."

HERMENEUTICS

Another area of interpretation of text comes from the field of hermeneutics, which we know best from the translation of the Bible from Latin to

English. Hermeneutics as a technique involved literally translating the first sentence from Latin to English. The scribe would then do a direct translation of the second sentence, then go back to the first translation, reinterpret, and rewrite the text given the new information of the second sentence. The meanings assigned to the translation considered both the context in which the translation occurred and the position of the translator. From this procedure it can be seen why it was such a rigorous process involving several layers of meaning dependent upon a constant returning to the text.

Initially, Husserl (1964) developed the philosophy in opposition to the dominant philosophy and positivistic methodology of science. Two major aspects of hermeneutics included eidetic reduction and eidetic variation. The word "eidetic" refers to vividness. In terms of Husserl's methodology, experience is reduced not only to its "lived" experience (phenomenology) but also to its vividness (including sensory and memory). The notion of eidetic variation involves the descriptive narrative under study.

One dramatic arts tradition that borrows from hermeneutic deconstruction belongs to chamber theater in which multiple variations of a text's meanings through time and space are presented. What has not traditionally been part of chamber theater is the application of Derrida's deconstruction methodology and other contemporary theories of interpretation supported by theories of cultural studies and criticism.

In drama, the notion of the hermeneutic approach can be seen as a way of understanding literature. While contemporary areas of interpretation (including postcritical, poststructural, and postmodern philosophy) encourage or, in fact, demand a plurality and fracturing of interpretations of the past, hermeneutic phenomenology encourages the reintegration and preservation of the textural meanings regarding the changes in language, contexts, values, and attitudes throughout time and space.

Philosophers of the hermeneutic tradition have developed variations on this initial attitude. Schleiermacher, Dilthey, Lukacs, Gadamer, Ricoeur, Habermas, and others have, each in their own way, added, rejected, or modified aspects of the traditional hermeneutic approach to the interpretation of text. Schleiermacher borrowed from and reinforced the romantic stress on the creative process of the imagination; Dilthey explored historical facts, events, and worldviews. Lukacs stressed the division within contemporary life that the act of imagination of alien experience had to overcome. Gadamer reinterpreted Aristotle's mimesis as play; Ricoeur added the flavor of psychoanalysis, being interested in the hermeneutics of demystification (decoding of the meaning presented to the interpreter in the form of a disguise). Habermas added the branch of hermeneutics associated with the critiques of social practice and cultural expression (Hilton, 1993). Overall hermeneutic phenomenology provides a range of possible approaches to the interpretation of texts through the dramatic arts.

RE-AUTHORING THE TEXT THROUGH DRAMA

In her book *Playing in the Dark: Whiteness and the Literary Imagination,* Toni Morrison (1992) discusses the taken-for-granted assumptions and the invisibility of Afro-Americans in literary imagination, products, and texts. Morrison claims that as a writer she struggles with language that can both evoke and make visible not only the experience of Afro-Americans, but also the hidden signs of racial superiority, cultural hegemony, and the marginalization of groups. She uses several examples of text to show that white authors neglect to privilege characters, plot, setting, or relationships based on race and color.

Morrison's best example of a construction of the literary imagination and how it is problematic for the author is the story *Sapphira and the Slave Girl.* In this story, a young black girl becomes the victim of a white mistress, who for lack of attention, encourages a white man to rape the black girl. The interesting feature of the story is the insertion of a seemingly irrelevant dialogue between the two black women (mother and daughter). Morrison shows how the dialogue passage contains "the silence of four hundred years . . . is out of the void of historical discourse on slave–parent–child relationships and pain" (Morrison, 1992, p. 22). The important feature about this passage for Morrison is that she recognizes not only the lack of elaboration or privileging of slave–parent–child relationships in the text, but the dependence of the author on the fact that blacks existed in the text to give a heroic plot and character to whiteness. "The master makes the slave work in order to satisfy his own desires" (Sarup, 1993, p. 18).

In the re-authoring of the text, Morrison privileges the slave–parent–child relationship, provides a language and a structure that no longer make assumptions or take for granted the experience of the Afro-American in the literary, and for our purposes, dramatic imagination of readers. In her books, such as *Jazz, The Bluest Eye, Sula, Tar Baby,* and others, Morrison recognizes the Afro-American experience, positions the reader, characters, experiences, and so forth as such, and thus privileges their lives. When we read Morrison, we first have to determine the position from which she is writing and how it positions Afro-American women historically, economically, and politically. Morrison shifts all our notions—she deconstructs as she writes—and moves us into oppositional reading and reading from a particular position. We resist the power, authority, and constructions that are so entrenched in our consciousness from a tradition of history books, family mythologies, popular culture, and cultural stereotyping. We do not have to deconstruct from our position necessarily; we are moved to a new position by the writer, in this case, Morrison. As different races read, they are moved closer to understanding the experiences of Afro-Americans.

The dramatic arts recognize that embedded within words and thoughts there are a host of relationships that are marginalized, silenced, or undervalued. When interpreting or using any texts for dramatization, the reader takes an in-role position as author from a different perspective, including many different cultural constructions. Repositioning requires an unpacking of the characters, plots, and settings, that is, re-authoring the text from an in-role presentation. If one were to go in-role as an author of a different gender, race, and/or political interest, the actors or audience (in-role) could then ask questions about what is missing, who should be privileged, and how the relationships should be constructed in a way that honors those seen originally as oppressed, devalued, marginalized, or invisible. Re-authoring might mean lifting a character out of the text, inserting a character based on the aforementioned qualities, and asking how this changes the authoring of the text.

In this free-authoring strategy, text forms in a dramatic mode act both as a challenge and a resistance to the construction of the dominant imagination. For example, in America, minority groups such as Afro-Americans, Puerto Ricans, Mexicans, Asians, homosexuals, lesbians, and physically and mentally challenged groups would be inserted back into the social imagination to provide compelling models for mapping out new constructions of relationships and political action in society. Challenge comes when we finally reinsert or privilege people, plot, experiences, truths, and relationships that are normally taken for granted.

With so much dismantling of the familiar there is "the risk of losing the reader's interest" (Morrison, 1992, p. 24). Even more challenging is that the consequences become a reworking and reconstruction of the social imagination. For example, if a white man were the accused rapist in *To Kill a Mockingbird,* and the lawyer were black, the text would need to be changed. The threat may become a lack of appeal to a white reader.

All constructions of law, social order, and community relationships are threatened in terms of the familiar world of the white reader in which plots are only of interest if the white reader becomes the hero through the heroics of a white lawyer.

A contemporary example is the movie *Philadelphia* (1994). The movie works because it appeals to knowledge and emotions, and because the hero is a man dying of AIDS. The antihero is a black lawyer. Two problematic issues arise in the dramatization of text. First, would the story have worked and been such a major box-office success if a heterosexual woman were dying of AIDS, and a woman lawyer were defending her? The other issue for the dramatization of text concerns the impact of the movie; that is, does it change people's attitudes (measured mostly by a change in people's actions)? Does the movie appeal to the vulnerability of the emotional center by sensationalizing the issue, or does it, indeed, evoke changes in people's everyday attitudes and actions toward the homosexual community? Is there a patronizing side effect from the audience, glad they never have to *really* live through this nor actually meet anyone who does?

When dramatizing text, whether from scripted text, novels, poetry, or informational content, an authentic reshaping of the world would come through a re-authoring of the text. In the play *Cut* (1985), characters who were "cut" by the writer's pen in the original plays, such as *Hamlet, The Importance of Being Earnest,* or *Death of a Salesman,* are moved to the foreground and included as major characters. Voice is given to these characters. We also see the world of the original text in a new way. What was silenced becomes voiced. What was invisible becomes seen. From this re-authoring of text, we have possibilities played out for a deconstruction and reconstruction of our thoughts and actions about social conditions, institutions, and people.

We could liken the re-authoring of a text to the literary strategies of parody and irony. A simple re-authoring, however, does not necessarily change our social imagination to rewrite the text and thus rewrite the world. The dramatic imagination informed by cultural studies and criticism explores and presents possibilities of the world through the re-authoring of text. If we practice drama as an agent of social change, we perform a rewriting of text in order to present a world that constantly moves, shifts, and crosses the boundaries of what the dominant culture defines as the norms. Both students of drama and text interpretation (whatever the text) need to be valued and evaluated, not purely for their theatrical ability, but for their ability to re-author the text through performance.

Other ways of re-authoring the text are through the insertion of marginal characters, neglected plot or devalued setting, and the reworking of the discourse of the text. Traditionally, drama used dialect as the major way of characterizing the world of discourse. It also used the language of "reality." When we re-author the text through discourse we have in mind the notion of "disengaging words from syntax, thus hindering the reconstruction of the 'projected world' " (McHale, 1989, p. 162). To subvert or resist the familiar is to subvert the discourse or, as McHale calls it, create an anti-discourse. We confront the unthinkable; it forces the audience to reflect on the discursive order of things.

Disengaging words from familiar syntax can happen in several ways. One way is to rearrange word order. As we "begin reflecting on the impossibility of such an order, we also come to reflect on the ideas of order which are possible for us to think" (McHale, 1989, p. 163). We undergo disorienting shifts from one world to another, placing us, as actors and as audience, with an uneasy juxtaposition of discourses.

Another way of performing a re-authoring of the text is through heteroglossia. This is a method of creating a multiple world of discourse by integrating a polyphony of voices, worldviews, and ideologies—"juxtapositioning and interweaving a variety of languages, styles, registers, genres and inter-textual citations upon the text" (McHale, 1989, p. 166). What we achieve through a polyphony of voices is a polyphony of worlds.

Text re-authoring also happens when we break up the closed discourse world of a univocal text and interject the discourse from other specialized discourses. Another means of breaking up the text, besides the disengaging of words from syntax or heteroglossia, is the strategy of antilanguage, which means the inclusion of "specialized discourse of a deviant social group . . . in the usual negative sense, such as criminal or imprisoned subcultures or . . . prestigiously deviant (e.g., military elites, religious mystics, perhaps even poets) (McHale, 1989, p. 168). Antilanguage is done through the adaptation of a standard word to nonstandard use or proliferation or synonyms of near synonyms. This, in turn, challenges standard language and dominant worldviews and creates, in effect, "an anti world view or a counter reality of its own that is dialectically related to straight or official reality" (McHale, 1987, p. 168).

Another strategy for breaking up text would be to "punctuate the collage of disparate genres and registers such as discourse from the field of obstetrics, popular magazines, disciplined textbooks or a government flyer although all on the same topic." The collage of discourse genres "heightens and foregrounds what could have been marginalized or taken for granted" (McHale, 1989, p. 169). The juxtaposition can be along a horizontal axis, a vertical axis, or a lamination. In the first, juxtaposition of discourses are placed end to end. In a vertical collage, two or more discourse worlds coexist within the same segment. A lamination or layering of discourses is when each segment belongs to two or more discourses.

Improvisation in some drama classes has perhaps, in an informal sense, created this re-authoring of our world. When students take familiar texts such as those from commercials or magazines and juxtapose them with a sacred text or a medical text, they have moved into multiple possibilities of reconstructing the conditions, thoughts, and attitudes of the original text. The frightening possibility here lies in the prophetical nature of the deconstruction and reshaping of the social imagination.

WHOSE INTERPRETATION SHOULD BE PRIVILEGED?

In a series of nature texts by Lyle Watson (1976), alternative relationships between humans and nature are portrayed. One story identifies how the natives of a Polynesian island relate to a beached whale compared to how a scientist and an environmentalist are studying the same phenomenon. Similar to most, if not all, aboriginal cultures, nature is everything and everybody. Unlike the Westernization of knowledge that separates humans from the natural environment, in the minds of aboriginals, animals, trees, air, and wind are not separate entities upon which humans inflict an objective knowledge or manipulate for human purpose and need.

In the case of the beached whale, Watson clearly demonstrates what happens when the knowledge of Western society is privileged over aboriginal knowledge. The environmentalist and the scientist study ways to weigh the whale, try to determine how it became beached, why whales do this, and how to get it back into the water. This is portrayed in stark contrast to the aboriginal way of knowing. The aboriginals see the beached whale as they would see anything or anyone in a state of near death. For the aboriginals what is of more concern than scientific knowledge is dignity in death. The aboriginals see the situation differently and act accordingly; what becomes important is to keep the whale moistened. In addition, an aboriginal girl chooses to sit with the whale, keep it moist, sing to it, and touch it in its last moments of life. From a Westerner's point of view this would most likely be interpreted as the wrong actions based on nonlegitimized or invalid knowledge. In other words, Western knowledge is privileged over that of aboriginal, rural, or Eastern knowledge.

The privileging of one group's knowledge over another is a phenomenon of the scientific way of knowing that has privileged the Western world since the Copernican revolution. At that time, humans became the center of the universe and knowledge was separated into objective and subjective. Even the scientific method that claims objectivity has crossed over into the human "sciences." Interestingly enough, arts and humanities have taken on this human sciences approach to knowledge and, in turn, to the interpretation of text. The privileging of the "sciences" as well as the modern privileging of technology means that the arts and humanities as knowledge or ways of knowing or thinking become marginalized, devalued, and, eventually over time, rendered obsolete. With this in mind, we begin the process of using the dramatic arts to privilege different knowledge. When texts use the theoretical perspectives of deconstruction and are driven by theories of poststructuralism, postmodernism, and postcolonialism, we can dismantle culturally constructed texts and then begin to privilege multiple knowledge, values, and so forth.

CHALLENGING ONE'S OWN IDEAS

Barthes (1986) talks of the resistant writer as one who challenges his or her own ideas. This statement has several implications for deconstruction, least of which is the recognition that each of our readings of a text is affected by whatever position of difference we speak from (gender, race, age, truth, experience, etc.). Previously in this chapter, deconstruction through the dramatic arts has assumed, although not intended, that text is derived only from such sources as script, novel, poetry, magazine, textbook, media, film, and so forth. Another source of text is oral narrative.

A variety of texts can be derived from interview, discussion, dialogue, and research on specific individuals and groups. For example, in a study of violence against women, students interviewed abused women living in transition homes. From this strategy, the students developed a performance piece based on the actual oral narratives of the women. Sometimes referred to as Collective Theater, this strategy allows the actors to select the aspects of the narratives that they wish to represent to an audience. Drama, as an agent of deconstruction, moves beyond the performance stage and opens doors to the audience who become, at the same time, participants.

Oral narrative as text requires the teacher, students, and/or actors to involve the creators of the text in the drama itself, not necessarily in final performance, but as a mode of reflecting on their knowledge and experiences. In this way, the creators of the text not only represent their world; they rehearse actions through reorganizing original texts and consciousness.

Boal (1985) uses text creators as the participants in the dramatic process. Through a series of strategies he developed, especially in his work with the peasants of Brazil, the actors reflect upon their own realities and texts. The three major formats Boal uses to do this are image theater, forum theater, and Theater of the Invisible. The participants act upon their text, first through the dramatic creation of their reality and then through intervention into that reality.

In a less formal way, drama can be used to engage the oral texts of subjects as possible transformation to performance. In the Canadian movie *The Company of Strangers,* the screenwriter and director interviewed a group of women with different life experiences. Their text formed the basis for the movie script, but they also became the actresses. The women, through their text, words, and worlds, were transformed into a medium that became subjective reflection on their lives and the lives of women. Both moviegoers and the actresses themselves were able to reflect on their experiences. What resulted from this dramatic strategy was that the words and experiences of the women were neither devalued nor forgotten, but transformed, illuminated, and elevated to a status of recognition. Perhaps in the representation of their experiences in the movie, the actors themselves were transformed or at least recognized for the value of their experience and wisdom. The audience is also transformed. By viewing the movie they realize that the everyday mundaneness of their personal and local texts are no longer taken for granted but are elevated to a status of validation and legitimacy.

When oral narratives are gathered, subjects participate in the dramatic organization and presentation of their own ideas, in this way creating an environment of reflexivity. Ideally, the audience should also do more than just view. They too could become part of the text through dramatic strategies such as those espoused by Boal, or through the turning back of the original interviews or research questions to the collectors of the data. In this way there is no end. The researchers collect oral text. The subjects who produce the oral text become part of the dramatic process, and in their presentation, the researchers are confronted with their own material. As a reflexive strategy it would assume that the purpose of the exercise would be to provide insights into the experiences and worlds of the subjects and allow a transformation of text as an agent of social change.

DRAMATIZATION OF TEXTS

Traditionally, the dramatization of texts, whether from literature or scripted plays, has involved a theater-voice approach or a speech-therapy approach. This chapter does not include acting techniques or speech exercises. It will, however, involve the implications of contemporary theories of drama, and text interpretation borrowed from the perspectives of deconstruction, cultural studies and criticism, poststructuralism, postmodernism, and postcolonialism. The intention is to move beyond traditional modes of text interpretation, such as literary criticism or performance scripts (including memorizing parts), and into the more cultural, political, and social implications filtered through the earlier-mentioned contemporary theories.

One of the sad side affects of our dependency on the printed word is that we have tended to devalue, and, in fact, even resist, the quality and energy that comes from an oral tradition. Oracy has diminished because of the heavy reliance on high-tech communication systems and on the printed word. In the dramatization of text taken mainly from the printed text, the privileging of the voice returns us to a connection between the voice as a major means of speaking our way into the world (Rodenburg, 1993).

What we can take from experts such as Rodenburg (1993) and Berry (1993) allows us to regain and give power to language and to text. Rodenburg states, "I believe that as you unlock a great oral text in the act of speaking it, you instantly connect across time to the writer writing the words onto paper . . . arousing a practical partnership between you and the writer of the text" (p. 96). The dramatization of text should balance the power of oracy, printed text, interpretation, and presentation in which no one area is sacrificed for the other.

While the language of science, "which assumes its own language [yet is] unaware of human existence" (Barthes, 1986, p. 8), enters a "gap of silence" (Steiner, 1982, p. 17), the educational impact of the dramatic arts is no longer meaningful, life-describing, or life-giving. Forgetful of the fullness of the descriptive qualities of language, the new languages began to dominate both the natural sciences and the human sciences. Prior to that period, "even the natural sciences were descriptive . . . and mathematical thought . . . was anchored to the material conditions of experience" (Steiner, 1982, p. 140). Language is no longer a life-giving language and no longer "a language that serves [their] lives" (Nietzsche, 1980, p. 4). "The voice is a thing of life, of energy" (Musashi, 1979, p. 79). It carries our existence.

If we dwell authentically in our lives and thus in our language, we remove the organization of the experience of mythical language from conceptual categories and "distortion by intellectual analysis" (Merleau-Ponty, 1962, p. 185). The oscillating density of oral language that emerges from the mythical experience flows with rhythm, meter, pitch, and unifies the speaker with the world. Although Plato's world of reason was suspicious of the rationalizing abilities of the oral poets, Aristotle felt spoken words were signs of the soul's experience.

Rebecca, a fifth-grade student, captures the textures of many lives by trying on different voices. The sounds of Rebecca's voice are impregnated with the technical cadence of the archaeologist's voice, the rhythms of the villager's daily life, the haunting hum of a poet's legend, and the tightened syllables of an Acadian mother's rage at impending separation from her children. The closer Rebecca's voice amalgamates with the voice of the mythical other, the more closely Rebecca participates in that life. Oral language serves to grant Rebecca entry into the unknown world of the Acadians.

Rebecca's experience is a recovery of the "rhapsodic intellect." The rhapsodes were singers of epic poems, the storytellers like Homer whose oral language wove together the message of the text. Oral language weaves a participatory life through the fibers of the voice. Sound evokes techniques of ecstasy (Eliade, 1964) like those of the shaman who chants life into another. Eagan (1987) calls for the oral foundations of education that would "immerse the young in enchanting patterns of sound until their minds resonate to them, until they become in tune with the institutions of their culture" (p. 451).

MURMURING THE BURDEN BACK

We speak in the mythical realm, in the world of possibility. The fullness of living in our language requires that we realize the dark side of life. These possibilities include the tragic, the repulsive, and the evil. Without the consideration of these elements in our lives, our understanding of the world becomes romanticized. We begin to avoid the queasiness of speaking about certain aspects of life. Furthermore, we direct our attention to the hedonistic and narcissistic culture by warding off that which disturbs and by ignoring the fullness of language and, thus, the fullness of life.

The title of this section, "Murmuring the Burden Back," is borrowed from the oral tradition technique of the aboriginal Ainu tribe of Japan (Berry, 1989). The burden is a constantly repeated refrain that carries the melody of Ainu epic narratives. As the stories of the Ainu are recited over and over again, the circle of listeners murmur the burden back; that is, the participants engage in the life of the story by reciting refrains that review the imagery, themes, and remembrances of the world (Philippi, 1982). I will use "murmuring the burden back" to describe the experience of weaving the tragic and evil threads of life through our language.

The experience of mythical language allows us the privilege of coming face to face with the tragic, repulsive, and evil of our lives. The stories of these burdens are contained in the mystery, wonder, and awe of our language, and in rhythms, tone, melody, and pitch of oral textures. In the innocence of our daily living and speaking lies the possibility for the emergence of the tragic and evil. When we truly hear in those open spaces of possibility, we can murmur the burden back; but, first, life stories must present themselves.

The freedom offered by the open spaces of the possible brings opportunities for living in the "hardships," and thus, in the language of hardship. In addition, the textuality of oral language deepens the dramatic experience. Granted, a variety of literary modes are embedded with the themes of evil and tragedy, but there is an added dimension of contact when we encounter the experience through the texture of oral language.

Dianne, a university student, researched the coal mining industry of Lethbridge, Alberta, Canada. She, like many of the students, found documents, books, films, and other resources on the topic. The students discussed the hardships of coal mining, especially the explosion that ended the industry. A major dramatic activity she engaged in was the interviewing of an eighty-year-old woman whose husband had died in that final explosion fifty years ago. Dianne, in-role, re-created the woman's memories of the last day with her husband even to the detail where her children sat in the bay window to wave goodbye to their father as he disappeared over a prairie hill to the coal mine. That moment—that murmuring of the burden back to the class—carried the entire historical struggle of the 1930s. The discourse of the woman found life through a dramatic presentation of her text, and Dianne carried that life to an audience for whom the burden of the Depression years was murmured back to us. Years later, that moment still resonates for all the students who were present, Shirley Steinberg included.

The power and dominance of men over women, whites over blacks, West over East, capitalism over socialism, Christians over Muslims, and the lack of access to the world based on physical and mental differences has a long way to go. We need only to look as far as our immediate everyday lives to see the measures of injustice. We can also look to the world scene predominantly through access given by television, film, and contemporary communication systems. When we look at the world through the lens of cultural studies, we can start to understand how the world works to structure privilege and oppression.

The project of the dramatic arts becomes one of how to institute actions and structures that reorganize the world. Drama as cultural studies has a part to play in that reorganization and creation of actions that move us toward a postcritical world. The hypothetical play, which is the nature of drama, provides an arena for students to begin both the recognition of oppression and the strategies with which to do something about it. When we "murmur the burden back" through the voice textuality and contexts of the dramatic arts, we reach a further point in the dismantling of modern cultural constructions.

THE O.J. SIMPSON TRIAL AS TEXT

One of the most prominent texts in 1995 was the O.J. Simpson trial. Within one week from the verdict announcement of "not guilty," the trial and, in a roundabout way, society, had already been deconstructed. The reason it is labeled as "the trial of the century," whether you agree or disagree with the verdict, is that it has upset many, while many others quickly became tired of it. I will use this trial as something with which, I assume, we are all familiar.

Popular culture is North Americans' major source of information and cultural constructions, knowledge, values, and actions. Popular culture is transmitted mainly through television and film media. North Americans are masters at it; there is no other nation that would lay itself as bare. Canada, however, does less so; it does not even allow cameras into its courtrooms. Mass media accesses texts for people to see; it makes accessible what used to be very elitist. From a cultural studies point of view, this is great. It gives one a whole text with which to work. If you watched television during this period, you would have seen how this trial was the subject of talks shows, situation comedies (sitcoms), news, and a multitude of other cultural sites. The reason seems to be that people "read the text" in different ways with dominant, negotiated, and oppositional or resistant reading—some with the grain, some against the grain.

Before and during the verdict, the O.J. trial was a media construction. Since the verdict, it has become a text for deconstruction. Actually the crime was reconstructed from all angles. Deconstruction of the O.J. text challenged race, wealth, privilege based on money, power, celebrity authority, the media, and the institutions that were represented.

A courtroom itself is a text and institution; so are law and forensic medicine. What about irony, that is, the perception of the justice system as just? Irony is an important part of postmodernism, and it addresses the issues of the power of class and wealth, and of capitalism (money made from residuals). Perhaps that is why, even today, the trial (like the Bill Clinton hearings) is the source for irony, parody, and jokes.

Some state governments have refused to allow people to profit from trial proceedings. In these states, rich people in jail cannot write books for profit. During Watergate and Irangate there were no such restriction; G. Gordon Liddy and Oliver North made millions. The watching of the O.J. trial made capital; it was seductive, hard to resist. Production is an issue in terms of popular culture. It was constructed in such a manner that made one desire, want, or "just have" to watch the trial. Many of us were completely seduced—many of us remained silent. Yet cultural critics and dramatists are by occupation required to use this text for deconstruction of cultural constructs.

There are so many surrounding cultural contexts of this trial that we, through in-role positioning, could challenge. The question of whether or not the media influenced the trial is a text in and of itself. Who determines who will be interviewed? In what order? With what questions? When we listen to interviews of differently positioned people and to the questions asked by differently positioned interviewers, we should recognize the theoretical implications and even ask the range of questions about the questioners and their deconstruction of the text.

Louis Farrakhan now has become part of the text because there are many aspects to deconstruct on him. Farrakhan, of "The Million Man March," is charismatic, an Afro-American male who is the leader of Afro-American Islam. Although he has been active for thirty years, he is now using the O.J. trial and the popular culture of media to bring forward his views. "The Million Man March" was a gathering of one million Afro-American men in celebration of their race. What is happening is people who do not follow his religion are questioning the validity of the march. People who are getting involved in the march are receiving some opposition. Multiple positions and readings are layered upon the Simpson trial.

Deconstruction, in its true sense, goes on forever. What happens with a text such as the O.J. trial are multiple readings, meanings, and positions. Even among the Afro-American community there were different

positions. What about women? We are making generalizations by constructing Afro-American women as one big group; within that group of
women are all kinds of differences. Oprah Winfrey is positioned differently from an Afro-American academic woman. The trial jurors were positioned differently while education was used as a position—literacy
became a reason for jury unsuitability and verdict delegitimization. Interestingly, it is the first time that a jury has ever been challenged or questioned. Also notable, if it had been a white jury, would literacy have been
an issue? Gates (1995) writes a rigorous article which clearly demonstrates that multiple readings of the trial are possible even within the
Afro-American community.

There are multiple texts and subtexts within the O.J. trial text. Fixed
thinking about the trial stays only within that realm; it feeds on itself and
does not go anywhere. To allow other readings from different perspectives to enter, the reading, writing, observing, or creating of text allows
changes to happen. In my location and as a dominant race that is different from those in the text under scrutiny, I cannot speak for nor understand others' positions, although I try and listen to the voices. However,
multiple meanings of a context moves us out of our own worlds.

DECONSTRUCTION OF TWO POPULAR MOVIES

The Piano (1994) offers many possibilities for investigation, interrogation, scrutiny, and dismantling. First there is the fixed fairytale ending. In
the final scene, on the porch, between Holly Hunter and Harvey Keitel,
the notion is perpetuated that women—because of men—live happily
ever after. Even in the 1800s, when the movie supposedly took place,
there were multiple endings to people's love stories. The standard Hollywood ending gave closure and, consequently, perpetuated the modern
construction of romantic love.

At the 1995 Canadian Learneds Conference in Montreal, six panel
members deconstructed *The Piano.* One of the women in the group
talked about classical music and how it plays on you as it is being played
during certain scenes and at certain moments; music becomes a subtext.
One woman read from a gendered position; one addressed race because
the representations of the aboriginal people in this text needed to be challenged. Another woman challenged gender from a male perspective; the
conflict here is the difference between her attempts versus a male's attempt. Other panel members read the text from the position of class, history, and colonialism.

I am opposed to the constructions of gender and race in this movie and to the representations of a colonial married to a colonized person. Harvey Keitel's role was foregrounded—he was used as capital because his reputation would sell the movie, while the aboriginal to whom he was married was pushed to the background. How could you represent that quite differently? Aboriginal people were put in a position of looking quite stupid, of not resisting or challenging, of being passive. I am sure aboriginal people would say that was not the way it was—there had to be resistance and challenge to colonization. If you rewrote, rescripted, or re-filmed the movie from several positions other than that of the preferred "Hollywood" reading, how would representations, structures, beginnings, endings, and cultural content be different? For instance, what about women during this time? What were they really doing?

In deconstruction, we have to hear many voices from many positions. Deconstruction becomes a polyphony of interpretations—multiple readings, beginnings, endings, and possibilities. We start to recognize, deconstruct, and oppose the preferred or dominant reading. If reading the film from a position of race, how would an oppositional reading deconstruct the meanings and structures within? From a gender position, a woman may have trouble with an ending that positions the male as having the last word, such as in *The River Wild* (1994) with the remark by the young son: "My mother is my hero but my dad saved our lives." If the movie had ended with "My dad saved us but my mom was the hero," would the audience accept a woman as a hero? Could Hollywood directors/screenwriters move beyond the familiar and the salable? A change in structure emits multiple readings, voices, interpretations, and points of view, and repositions women as heroes (although the problem is that heroism is still being defined by men's roles).

BACKLASH AGAINST DECONSTRUCTIONISM

It appears when we deconstruct and say that there are other avenues, we ignore what has been the norm for so long and say that it is not acceptable. Deconstruction offers multiple readings; it is not that something is right or wrong when we begin to value others nor do the traditional values become less valued. If the traditional, nuclear, or extended family is the dominant or preferred content and structure of family, then several other possible family constructions are excluded or devalued, thus limiting the idea and practice of family life. In addition to the modern construction of family being exclusive, it remains subject to hegemonic practices that serve public and state institutional apparatuses such as the school, church, and government. Policies and discourses bend truths and constructions and thus, in turn, legitimize themselves.

Deconstruction of a text under scrutiny attempts to dismantle the dominant, fixed notions of what constitutes a family. Currently, a dominant preferred reading is that youth violence is increasing because women are not staying home, which is causing the loss of the nuclear family, that is, the family that is made up of a man, a woman, and children. Dominant readings do not recognize that there are other possible constructions of family that have to be valued as well. When we start to value others, we are trying to reach an equilibrium so everyone receives equal treatment. And how do we value without devaluing the traditional?

We don't. As Nietzsche (1980; also see Chapter 1) states, we use and abuse three aspects of history: the monumental, the ancestral, and the critical. The issue is, what do we keep and what do we throw out? Related to constructions of family, we say, "There is a family construction that happens to be the dominant one right now." We make decisions and policies; we construct, educate, and socialize people based on a preferred textual construction of family. However, who is excluded, voiceless, powerless? What silences are dangerous? What needs to become public and thus political? Spousal abuse? Child abuse? What does it mean for recognition of homosexual families? Women who want choices outside the home? We want to show and value other kinds of constructions of family life. In the dominant mode, we exclude; "we" includes ourselves, institutions, welfare, and government decisions.

Part of the backlash against the feminist movement is couched in hegemonic discourse. Feminists devalue motherhood. Feminists devalue nuclear families. Feminists claim all women should work outside the domestic realm. These and many similar statements are backlash statements that serve a particular stance and close the doors on the history of family, women, children, and men, and the possibility of alternative constructions of family life.

Indeed, as a critical theorist could claim—this is the political discourse of far-right conservatism—or as Nietzsche might claim, the use of history to celebrate the nuclear family as monumental and ancestral. But to neglect the critical and allow (excuse the pun) the abuse of women and children in the family structure without dismantling the constructions that are abusive serves only to continue the hegemonic practices.

There are so many different positions from which we speak. If I read "women staying at home and not being paid for it," then I say that women are not being valued. It is problematic because they have to stay in that position because they have no power outside the realm of the domestic and, quite arguably, very limited power within the domestic arena (physically, economically, educationally, politically). When women stay home and do not get an education, they do not have the power to make choices outside that situation or to leave that situation. If women do not have economic power, then they have to stay in abusive relationships. This does not devalue the stay-at-home mom; it devalues the fact that such women have no economic power and no choices. I am not reducing women to just economic power, but that is one aspect. And as to the romantic notion of family, we must turn to history and realize that notions of love and the nuclear family as romantic is a construction of modern life and does not necessarily fit or legitimize the current dominant constructions of family.

Feminist theory, whatever the slant, has been a major factor in the dismantling of modern constructions of family yet the major political voice that has directed attention to the valuing of women in both the private and the public sphere. As for empowering men, women without economic or educational power are dependent on men, which places men in a particular position. If men do not earn the money, they can be put down and made to feel guilty. Modern institutions, however, value male knowledge and structures. If they valued women who want to remain solely in the domestic realm, it would be possible for those women to have that choice with powers within and outside the domestic realm. Subsidized universal day care, for example, gives women that choice—an early agenda of the feminist movement. We have not done that because we have not allowed this choice to be valued by others. Multiple readings and possibilities mean that decisions do not have to be exclusive or alien, just multiple choices.

Limitation to nil choice becomes a means of keeping people in their places and affecting movement or change. It seems that when we deconstruct and tear down a construction, we have to tear down everything with it. One can say, "I'm a homosexual person. I can make this choice." Previously, and still in many contexts today, a homosexual person did not have choices or political agency. Backlash, whether everyday gossip or political discourse, serves only to eliminate or abuse the drives and desires of what deconstructionists steer, the dismantling of modern realities in order for multiple realities to be constructed and from which humans can choose what is right for them. Cultural constructions that are brought into the political arena for deconstructive dismantling offer steps forward, not backlash.

DECONSTRUCTION THEORY IN DRAMATIC ACTION

The following is an example of a studio class that uses theories and practices of cultural studies and deconstruction, to interrogate and dismantle different texts. Thirty-two students are in four groups. Each group selects a text. Texts are gathered from everyday life, personal experience, films, scripts, television, books, newspapers, history textbooks, and a host of other sources of cultural constructions. Possible examples available range from fertility and playground behavior to school report cards and therapy. The students create a three-minute text. If it is "playground," they do a playground scenario. (If in-role as children, do not act as you think children might act, since adults in-role as children tend to patronize or dishonor the intelligence and integrity of children.) Include dialogue and action. If, for example, the scenario is a therapy text, have people waiting in the office, the secretary there, and the family going in for therapy. In drama, keep it simple!

On a piece of paper, write the word "identity." Identify who you are in-role in the scenario. For example, you could say that you are a teacher, male, and give your age, class, education, and a general history—give as much information about your in-role self as you can. You have to have a history when you go in-role. Fold the paper up as small as you can and hold it in your hand. This is to remind you to stay in-role during the scenario and during any dramatic strategies that are used before, during, or following the three-minute scenario (such as hot-seating, halved soul, inner voices, voice-overs, corridors, forum theater, and so on). Further excellent dramatic strategies for interrogation and dismantling dramatic strategies can be found in Boal (1985), Heathcote (in Wagner 1976), Neelands (1990), O'Neill and Lambert (1976), Booth and Lundy (1985), and many others.

Each individual student also pulls from a hat one of the tenets of cultural studies (see Chapter 3) in order to deconstruct the scenario: power, discourse, homogeneity, representations, positioning, institutions, resistance, subject construction, structures, truths, knowledge, history, borders, margins, values, individualism, hegemonic practices, or any other words on which each member of the audience could focus during the scenario performance.

Each group presents its scenario. Encourage the actors to hold tightly onto their pieces of identity so they will stay in-role even under pressure of interrogation. Concentration is hard. If you were doing this exercise with your students, you could have them wear name tags to identify their subject roles. If they were going in as a subject construction, for example, a monk, they could wear something to signify a monk (a cross). (In grades 3, 4, and 5 this seems to work very well.)

Each group will present a scenario. Each member of the audience has a particular tenet or element of cultural studies through which she or he reads the text. If you have "power," you will look at power structures of discourse in the scenario. If you have "discourse," you could copy down some of the statements that are power statements. Some can be very subtle, like "Well, yes, dear." "Dear" is a power word because it places somebody in a particular way. You will listen and look for cultural constructs that are very familiar, unfamiliar, concrete, abstract (such as truth, knowledge), that are standard, taken for granted, and assumed natural. How is this knowledge, truth, and history created, maintained, and circulated without challenge and with consensus (hegemony)? How is so-and-so positioned to somebody else in terms of power? What institutional structures are in play in this? What kind of resistance is there and to what? Resistance comes in all shapes and sizes; even silence can be a resistance.

Each actor has in hand an identity. When representing males, represent the subject construction called "maleness." What subject constructions are there of gender, race, class, and so on? What is that person representing? Why do they walk this way? You will look at the structure of the scenario in terms of beginning, middle, and end. What is the content? What knowledge is being portrayed? For example, "I think that 50 percent of the population is . . . " is a knowledge legitimized by statistics. About truths, what are we accepting as truths? For example, "Mary, you play that because girls know how to skip" is something we have accepted as a truth. What is being valued in the scenario in terms of material things or beauty? What values, people, knowledge are being pushed to the margins? What are the borders of the playground other than the physical ones? For example, what kind of historical constructs have brought this to this point? (For example, sixth-grade girls as spectators of sixth-grade boys' playground sports.)

When you have a sense that someone is marginalized, being silenced, excluded, or put down into a position of powerlessness and they do not resist or nothing is said, look for this as a hegemonic practice. It is unchallenged power. Hegemony is the acceptance of the status quo, consensus, going along, getting along. Ask how it maintains and circulates in that text and context? What are the reasons of the personal, everyday, group, institutional, political, and public realm that sustain and circulate hegemonic practices?

Number the scenarios from 1 to 4. Each audience member remains focused on the particular element of cultural studies chosen from the hat, so that there is no observation overlooked. Don't forget there are several assumptions, for example, the text is a traditional history lesson being taught in a classroom. There are males and females of different races, countries, and religious or ethnic backgrounds in the group. Take a couple of males outside talking at the lockers in the hallway: One says, "Gee, those Greek battles were really great." The women would be saying, "History's just all those guys fighting."

Several strategies can be applied during or after the scenario is presented, although the most effective is to use dramatic, cultural studies, and deconstruction strategies during the performance (see Chapter 6). Too many stops, freeze-frames, or interruptions during the performance can burden or bore both the participants and the audience. For example, one such strategy used during a scenario that deconstructs the mythological history of male-constructed stories is what I call the "halved-soul," borrowed from the book called *The Halved Soul* by Judith Pintar (1992). What she does is retell stories, like the story of Adam and Eve. Just as the story begins, a character called Lilith appears and demands of Eve, "Now you've seen this story; do you know what's happening to you? Do you realize what's going on here?" Lilith shows Eve how she has been oppressed by the Adam and Eve story. *The Halved Soul* is actually how we have constructed romantic love. In this book, love is being deconstructed from a feminist position; the persona Lilith is traditionally seen as the "bitch." Lilith tells Eve that there are other sides to this story, to look at where it has positioned her, to look at the power—to reposition the knowledge, truths, history, and so forth, of women.

After the scenario, ask of the actors (in-role), "Do you know what was happening to you and what was going on?" "Hot-seating" can be addressed to the person to whom it is referring. We will do "halved soul" first; we will tell the actors (in-role) what was happening to them. Then, we will use the technique of hot-seating. A strategy like hot-seating is why the actors really need to hold onto the "identity" piece of paper. We will ask, "What's wrong with you? Why didn't you do something about it? Why did you say that? "Hot-seating" is so named because one is put under this kind of questioning, challenge, scrutiny, or interrogation until the seat gets too hot. Remember to whom you are addressing the challenge; actors remember to stay in-role.

AN EXAMPLE OF A STUDIO SESSION
OF DECONSTRUCTION

The following is an excerpt from another actual studio session. This was the first attempt at deconstruction of text through dramatic strategies where the text was a family mealtime—single mother, two children, and an elderly parent of the mother:

Audience member #1: I'm addressing the mother. Why did you not have people in the family help you do your chores? Why did you do all the meals?

Professor: Sorry, but you're hot-seating first instead of halved-soul strategy. First ask what they see. For example, "Did you notice you were always doing this?" Make it nonconfrontational to begin, bring actor to awareness of her or his portrayal before you use the hot-seat or halved-soul strategy.

Audience member #1: Did you notice that your family was questioning you when you said you were the one who was going to do all the meal preparing?

Professor: Who are you going to address it to? What are the myths that the actors are working with?

Audience member #1: The mother has everyone address everything to her. I don't know how she got it but she seemed to have the power. No one was going to buy anything without her consent.

Professor: So what you're really addressing is "Did you notice that the mother had all this power?" What you're saying is that these people were obviously not aware of this and you're now making them aware of power.

Audience member #1: About money, about things that they wanted; they all went to her. Also, the children knew who was going to clean up, who was going to cook the meals.

Audience member #2: Did you notice that it wasn't even questioned when the grandmother and mother left the table? The responsibilities were accepted by the mother totally without challenge. No challenge was given to the grandmother at all. It was just accepted how the grandmother was treating the whole family. "I'm not finished yet." "I want my bath now." "It would be better if we got another bathroom." She seemed very in control.

Audience member #3: My element was value. I looked at values of the family. The mother seemed to be the one who needed all that attention. She provided magazines but she made sure they were magazines she thought were appropriate. Money was a value they discussed and considered because one of the girls wanted to be socially accepted by the other kids in the class. That was the value that she prized. The mother wanted the attention because of the way her mother made her; the grandmother depended on that one daughter. I wondered if they had seen *Like Water for Chocolate* (1993). That's what I thought the whole time I watched mother and grandmother talking to each other.

Audience member #4: I had subject construction. I felt it was a very middle-class Western-style family. The gender roles were very traditional as far as the son and the daughter, the wife, and the grandmother were concerned.

Professor: You must identify from what position you are reading the text— white middle-class woman, white middle-class male, English, nonnative, and so on. Remember your little piece of paper? What cultural studies and deconstruction do that is different from critical analysis is that they identify what positions they're reading from that would influence their readings and meanings. If you say that you're reading from the position of a white middle-class female of an Afro-American text, then it will be different from an Afro-American person reading it. Afro-Americans are positioned differently; they have different experiences, histories, language, points of view, investments. Identify who you are when you deconstruct. I talk differences because I obviously have been influenced. Gender I can talk about. I can talk about race from the privilige of my whiteness. I can talk about being a differently abled person who has been oppressed and marginalized. Another thing that you assume is that you are not speaking for all white middle-class people nor are you giving the only reading possible.

Audience member #3: The fact that you state from what position you are observing and accept multiple readings of this text differs from analysis.

Professor: That's right. Position influences your reading, your meanings, and how you position others.

Audience member #3: So does that mean that we're only supposed to look at the text from one position?

Professor: It would be hard to read it from an unfamiliar position. If Heather is going to read it with Brian, she's positioned as a female and Brian is positioned as a male because that will influence the readings also.

Audience member #3: If you're watching something and you had an experience that is different from something that is taking place?

Professor: You state that. You make it explicit that that is the position from which you are reading. Give the multiple readings that the group has. If you're doing it as one person, you would identify who you are and state your position, for example, gender.

Audience member #3: Then you don't do them all; you don't read for all the exclusions?

Professor: That would be too many. If doing it by yourself, stick to one area; otherwise you can't get deep into the hidden kinds of things that you never would have thought of; if you just touch all of them on the surface, that's all you do.

This probing of the dramatic text with questions, comments, and readings of the text from different positions and so forth managed to move these novices into a comfortable arena of drama and doing deconstruction. Each question borrowed from cultural studies and each dramatic strategy allowed a ludic deconstruction of the text, a gift from the playfulness of the dramatic rehearsal process.

CHAPTER 5

Hegemonic Resonances

Throughout the previous chapters, several theories and themes of cultural studies and criticism were introduced as background to contemporary thinking and practices. The major functions were to interrogate and dismantle modern cultural construction specifically through the dramatic arts. Modern life is the source of cultural constructions that have become problematic at the *fin de siècle* and serve as text and structure for the application of contemporary theories. Several cultural studies themes have been excluded. Two major areas, however, that have constructed modern consciousness are history and hegemony; the former will be discussed in the framework of theories of hegemony that, in essence, leaves modern life unchallenged. The concept of hegemony is a major contributor to the complacency and acceptance of modern-day cultural constructions, especially in the capitalist, bourgeois-dominated world of Western culture.

CONCEPTUAL DEFINITIONS OF HEGEMONY

The concept of hegemony embodies many aspects and has no borders. What remains is a web of meanings with several political threads that weave through the definitions. Originally, the word "egemonia," as used by the Greeks, meant the predominance of one state over another, which would be relevant at the time to the political complexity and struggle of the disunified Greek states. In recent modern times, the concept has been included as a force and strategy for winning the support of the masses throughout historical and political upheavals. For our use in the dramatic arts, I will explore the concept as a theoretical tool for understanding additional dimensions of modern constructions in order to rehearse transforming them.

One of the simplest definitions is given by Thwaites and Mules (1994): "Hegemony is a social process of consensus in which power relations follow the cultural leadership of a dominant group" (p. 128). Other authors, however, argue that hegemony is not a totality of agreement about state or ruling-class power, but more of a social "consent" by the masses. A lengthier description by Holub (1992) introduces some of the complexities of social processes that add depth to our interest in hegemony as a tool for the deconstruction of modern contexts. Holub's definition is as follows:

> Hegemony is a concept that helps to explain, on the one hand, how state apparatuses, or political society—supported by and supporting a specific economic group—can coerce, via its institutions of law, police, army and prisons, the various strata of society into consenting to the status quo. On the other hand, and more importantly, hegemony is a concept that helps us to understand not only the ways in which a predominant economic group coercively uses the state apparatuses of political society in the preservations of the status quo, but also how and where political society and, above all, civil society, with its institutions ranging from education, religion and the family to the microstructures of the practices of everyday life, contribute to the production of meaning and values which in turn produce, direct and maintain the "spontaneous" consent of the various strata of society to that same status quo. (p. 6)

It was during the early part of the twentieth century that Gramsci, an Italian philosopher imprisoned for his political resistance to the Fascist dictatorship, revitalized and extended the definition of hegemony from a strategy to a conceptualized political theory. He moved hegemony beyond the revolutionary use by Lenin and Marx to a realm of ideologies and social practices defined by Gramsci as

> intellectual and moral leadership (*direzione*) whose principal constituting elements are consent and persuasion. A social group or class can be said to assume a hegemonic role to the extent that it articulates and proliferates throughout society cultural and ideological belief systems whose teachings are accepted as universally valid by the general populations. Ideology, culture, philosophy, and their "organizers"—

the intellectuals—are thus intrinsic to the notion of hegemony. (Fontana, 1993, p. 14)

Gramsci reinstates hegemony into mainstream structures that, in turn, mobilize intellectuals as the "organizers" of consent. He is the theorist of consent as legitimization (Sassoon, 1983, p. 123). Discursive struggles, that is, those that are achieved by taken-for-granted processes, acquire cultural authority, brought into play by "moral and philosophical leadership, leadership attained through the active consent of major groups in a society" (Femia, 1981, p. 28). Opposition and conflict is neutralized by hegemonic processes, guided by intellectual leadership, maintained and circulated with the "organic" masses' consent. Strategies employed by the dominant groups involve discursive negotiations and institutional maneuvering whereby the governed—the practical consciousness—shift their oppositions and conflicts to what, it seems, are those of the governing group.

What is amazing about Gramsci's theory of consent is that process for the dominant is achieved by a combination of coercion and persuasion, not force; hegemonic discourse, not dictatorial rhetoric; construction of ideological and political consent, not voting; self and civil organization more so than state organized; and, finally, active consent, not passive apprehension. Grounded in "consciously interventionist thought" (Williams and Williams, 1993, p. 152), theories of hegemony, especially in supposedly democratic societies, create sites of cultural formations for interrogation and dismantling. Awareness of hegemonic apparatuses, discourses, and structures, institutional and bureaucratic organization and policies, and state and civil integration is a key factor in understanding the rise and fall of a whole body of structures, superstructures, and practices in which "one concept of reality is diffused throughout society in all its institutional and private manifestations, informing with its spirit all taste, morality, customs, religious and political principles, and all social relations, particularly in their intellectual and moral connotations" (Salamini, 1981, p. 136).

Hegemony is present in all cultural constructions ranging from family to school, from gender to race, from church to government, from literature to media, and finally, from self to world. Dominant ideologies and structures become legitimized, thus privileging the ruling group's truths, knowledge, and values which the "masses" consent to, but are not privy to, because of many closed avenues (e.g., economy, education, discourses, history, religion, race, class, and so forth). Interrogation of power relations are most likely created, determined, manipulated, circulated, and maintained by a ruling class and sustained by the active consent of the nonruling class through the application of hegemonic apparatuses.

As Knight et al. (cited in Usher, 1994) propose, the employment of Gramsci's "Theory of Consent" in the study of two conflicting Australian curriculums about racism and multiculturalism becomes "a model of social life that is concerned with the way in which power, including systematically structured relations of domination and subordination" (p. 136) is mobilized. Furthermore, the dramatic arts as a process of exploration, informed by and directed by contemporary cultural studies and criticism, acts hegemonically as conscious interventionist thought. Although the rehearsals and ludic processes of the dramatic arts and application of hegemonic theory seem like strange bedfellows, both complement the "evolving sphere of superstructural conflict in which power relations are continually reasserted, challenged, modified, [and activated]" (Williams and Williams, 1993, p. 152) as a process of a "historically emergent project of restructuration . . . [with] different forms in different social formations and national contexts" (Grossberg, 1992, p. 244). Perhaps Adamson (1980) best summarizes the intent of a marriage between the dramatic arts and theories of hegemony, each allowing us "to recast the issues of social identity and social groups in the light of societal inequality" (p. 100).

Personally, I am most interested in using theory of hegemony as a tool to dismantle cultural constructions especially in the contexts in which I use the dramatic arts and with the subjects whom I teach. Most critical studies and criticism work in the dramatic arts is with oppressed and working-class students such as that of Boal (1985), Kershaw (1992), and others. Since most of my teaching is with Canadian, European-descent, middle-class university students, dominance, oppression, marginalization, and hegemony do not seem as relevant to present as it might be to those working with Theater of the Invisible, and so forth, for example, with mainly bourgeois, white teachers. For example, at a Toronto Council of Ontario Drama Educators conference in 1987, there were such levels of discomfort, not from dramatic contact with the subject under study, but from intellectual, middle-class apathy and cultural disinterest, that Boal's work was scorned or shrugged off. I feel that what my students seem to take for granted about culturally constituted worlds (including our own) is packed with power relations that surround them constantly, consistently, and discursively. Power, in a dominant middle-class world, is exposed and recognized by the application of theories of hegemony (as espoused by Gramsci) and the dramatic arts, which include improvised scenarios, oral-narrative dramas, and scripted texts. In this way, we all undertake the task of bringing contemporary theories to dramatic worlds as being culturally constituted, exposing their inequalities and injustices, and bringing to bear conditions of possibility and change.

HEGEMONY AS CONSCIOUS INTERVENTION

If hegemony requires consent without force or coercion, how does Gramsci see the process occurring? To him, it is an interactive process among what he terms "organic intellectuals" (i.e., those men and women who have the interest and capacity to organize society at moral and philosophical levels). Similar to his predecessors, Marx and Lenin, Gramsci was concerned with the relationship between power and the state. Unlike his predecessors, who emphasized economics and materialism's revolution, Gramsci brought the hegemonic process into the realm of education and the "organic" intellectuals as the leaders of society instead of the common knowledge of the masses. The influence of history, traditions, mythologies, entrenched memories, and formal and informal absorption of knowledge, truths, and values from both the private and public environment shape conscious thought as common sense, "which tends to make [people] accept inequality and oppression as natural and unchangeable" (Simon, 1982, p. 26). Hegemonic processes work to "create new ideological terrain, . . . a reform of consciousness and . . . methods of knowledge" (Golding, 1992, p. 108). Without the organizing principles of the intellectuals, common sense remains static, uninformed, arbitrary, and disparately subject to organization by military and state force and coercion. The struggle for the organic intellectual is to identify and consciously intervene in the thoughts and "common sense" philosophy of men and women that are often confused and contradictory.

In Gramsci's philosophy, education extends beyond the traditional boundaries of institutionalized schooling, which is run mainly by the state and church curricula. Gramsci's formulation of cultural sites as "schools" is advantageous in the following way:

> The advantage of conceiving all societies, including existing bourgeois societies, as "schools" is that we become alerted to the multiple contexts in which legitimation processes occur and, conversely, in which alternative political outlooks can be prepared. Moreover, it allows such

lofty socialist goals as an "autonomous and superior culture" or a
"total integral civilization" to be concretely mediated by present educational programs. (p. 142)

This theoretical synthesis between school and life complements the intentions of this book whereby all cultural constructions drawn from everyday
life are subject to interrogation and dismantling strategies contained
within the ludic processes of the dramatic arts. In addition, the dramatic
arts as a pedagogical art, more than as presentation or performance-
oriented arts, connect Gramsci's theory of hegemony with the vast array
of contemporary theories available in cultural studies and criticism, thus
permitting if not demanding that any field where dramatic arts are played
becomes a "school." And not "school" as the institutional context, which
state or church have dominated for centuries. And not pedagogy as it has
been used to mean education, child-centered, teacher-facilitated, subject
discipline, or any of a plethora of "schooling" discourse that places, at
any time, teacher, student, or knowledge as the powerful and dominant
center. I use *pedagogy* as does Max Van Manen (1991)—"the transformation of consciousness that takes place in the intersection of three
agencies—the teacher, the learner, and the knowledge they together produce" (p. 3)—and as does David Lusted—"pedagogy refuses to instru-
mentalize these relations, diminish their interactivity or value one over
another. It, furthermore, denies the teacher as neutral transmitter, the student as passive, and knowledge as immutable material to impart. Instead,
the concept of pedagogy focuses attention on the conditions and means
through which knowledge is produced" (see Grossberg, 1992, p. 15).

What some refer to as "cultural workers" (Freire, 1994, Giroux, 1991,
Shor and Freire, 1987), Gramsci calls "organic" intellectuals. In other
words, "organic" refers to the role in which intellectuals can mediate between the common sense of subaltern people and the dominant, ruling,
bourgeois class. In the alteration of consciousness through pedagogical intervention, intellectuals are responsible and capable of remaining tied to
the "organic" common sense of the people, and in close touch with their
knowledge, thoughts, interests, and needs. In Adamson's (1980) words, we
find the sense that intellectuals are not an exclusive class drawn from the
ivory towers of academia, or as an intellectual aristocracy; in capitalism

> the organic intellectuals are not just the specialists in management and
> industrial organization, the economists, the doctors, and the lawyers, but
> also the journalists, publishers, television personnel, and everyone else
> associated with what is now sometimes called the "culture industry." In

the case of the proletariat under capitalism, one would include as organic intellectuals all those striving to create a new proletarian culture as well as production functionaries in a narrower sense, such as shop foremen, machine technicians, and trade union economists. (p. 143)

In the case of a subaltern class like the proletariat, organic intellectuals seek to inspire its self-confidence as a historical actor and to provide it with social, cultural, and political leadership (p. 143). In other words, by providing intellectual-moral guidance and inspiration, the function of this type of leadership is an organization of "collective intellectuals" (Bogg, 1976) able to interrelate the economic, political, and cultural ideologies of the masses, not to a state of consensus, but of consent. This organization of collective individuals would also remain "rooted in the structure in a way that would both become its expression and, at the same time, maintain an *organic* [emphasis mine] relation to that structure" (Golding, 1992, p. 110). The revolution becomes an intellectual revolution, not a military or state war. The revolution is led by civil society, but is not removed from the cultural elites of state society, and it becomes counter-hegemonic in light of the existing hegemony.

HEGEMONY AND SUBJECT CONSTRUCTION

What should strike the reader as odd at this point in the presentation of hegemony as a theory of consent is that in the context of the contemporary theories discussed previously there seems to be conflict and contradictions. On the one hand, cultural studies and criticism seem to be theories of difference, whereas, on the other hand, hegemony is a theory of consent that seems to eliminate or hide differences. In the twentieth century, the rise of individualism in which an individual is constructed by selecting and making free choices about self was a dominant philosophy. Sartre and other existentialists claimed the individual existed in itself and for itself—that is, *en soi/pour soi*. Another major counterpoint to contemporary theories of culture and hegemony is the argument used by the essentialist. Individuals are born that way, which leaves the support of essentialism in tact. According to the essentialist argument, people, structures, institutions, gender, and sexuality for example, have some fundamental essence; that is, "essence implies a claim that there are some characteristics—essential characteristics—which are possessed by certain objects such as social, economic formations, or by human beings, which exist independently of the discourses or theories which construct them" (Bocock, 1986, p. 112). However, "the criticisms turn on the claim that no such essences can be established outside of any discourse. It is language and its associated practices which construct 'essence,' and it is therefore better to make this clear by avoiding any talk about an inner essence, such as human nature or even the essential characteristics of a mode of production" (Bocock, 1986, p. 112).

Another important point to consider is the strong influence of the outside world on the consciousness of the individual. If, indeed, subject construction were an individual essence or was separate from the social world, differences between humans would not exist (i.e., choice would make us "essentially" human beings, thus grounded, perhaps, in biology and genetics) engineered by the power given through scientific disciplines. Cultural studies and criticism become not a "natural selection" by the individual, but a study of "the dialectic between individual consciousness and structural determinants" instead (Becker and McCall, 1988).

Indeed, the subject as historically constituted is "subjected" to the hegemonic process with individual consciousness being shaped as a social identity; choice is not individual but group, either by force or consent. Identity replaces, although not in a totalizing way, individualism and is appreciative of "the diversity of the socio-cultural discursive practices from which identities are woven . . . and account/s [for] identity construction which . . . accounts for identity shifts over time" (Adamson, 1980, p. 107).

Much of educational and theater arts discourse is entrenched with psychologisms that structure modern life including people as individuals and in turn becomes a taken-for-granted condition restricting people to "do your own thing," "express yourself," "find yourself," "self-concept," "self-discipline," and volumes of other rhetoric. In this discourse, cultural identity and influence are neglected or invisible, which shifts responsibility and freedom totally to the individual and removes any responsibility and action on the part of people. This crisis of individualism or the constitution of the person as individual encourages the dominance of self-help books, groups, and organization. What is definitely problematic here is the lack of political focus and action (i.e., a lack of commitment or investment in the "self-help" structure to organize politically for power).

The idea that human subjectivity is constituted not by self or naturally but by cultural artifacts and the realm of the symbolic—that is, "not as purely linguistic reference but as involving material practices, rituals, and institutions" (Bocock, 1986, p. 107)—allows cultural studies to follow or deconstruct the process involved in the constitution of subjectivity by cultural forces, including that of hegemony. For these cultural forces to be effective and reach a point of consent that shapes the identity of the constituted subject and thus hegemony, individuals must identify (and resist) with particular positions, including the discourses, institutions, and the entire range of the symbolic ordering of culture and people.

In the dramatic arts, explorations of human subjectivity as subjected to external forces are the focus of work like Heathcote's (in Wagner, 1976) and Boal's (1985)—unlike most modern dramatic arts that focus on individualism, where outside the dramatic text the directors, actors, designers, crew, playwrights, and the character as individual-in-role receive as much attention as the content or process of the art form. We know more about Shakespeare and Hamlet as individuals than we do of the historical and cultural process including hegemony of the times in which the text was constructed. Both Heathcote and Boal work with subjectivity as historically and culturally constituted. They apply dramatic strategies specific to their theories; they deconstruct human subjectivity (not characters as individuals) and hegemonic processes; and they build interest and obsession (and thus learning) in the content and political consciousness. Heathcote mainly does so discursively, whereas Boal is more explicit. More importantly, subjects as political agents of change and power are examined. Heathcote's strategies of teacher-in-role and mantle-of-the-expert are two major and valuable contributions to the dramatic arts, especially as group processes and education. What remains in regard to hegemony is how subjects become (or not become) political agents through positioning, resistance, historical consciousness, memories, popular culture, and metaphors of hegemony.

AGENCY

To mobilize subjects through hegemony grants them an active participation in the making of history and production of culture. From a previous section in this chapter, it was evident that Gramsci saw education by intellectuals as capable of systemizing, coordinating, and maintaining consent in the disorganized, commonsense thoughts and desires of the masses or the ruled. Gramsci, however, saw the world as "school," but as Femia (1981) states about previous critical philosophers, they felt that "active man-in-mass lacks . . . education to manipulate abstract symbols . . . and [that] all the institutional mechanisms . . . schools, church, political parties, mass media, trade unions . . . in one way or another play into the hands of the ruling groups" (p. 44).

Such a perspective makes human agency very important to both hegemonic and counter-hegemonic practices—difficult but important. With the "emphasis upon agency, upon consent, and upon political will, in order to both understand and to achieve change" (Bocock, 1986, p. 120), education becomes political. Subjective consciousness is educated as a moral and cultural force, informed of material conceptions of power and hegemony and empowered through systematized reflexivity in order to "act both individually and collectively to change the conditions" (Lather, 1991, p. 4).

The exercise of hegemonic practices to achieve power for the ruling classes is easily accomplished if the common classes are kept uninformed, do not resist, or are coerced by power of state force, not civil law. In spite of education, the ruling class(es) may place "organic intellectuals at strategic points within the cultural and ideological 'apparatus' and will make alliances with the most influential traditional intellectuals" (Adamson, 1980, p. 149). So human subjects may still lose their power, to be active, to be agents of the power to create, initiate, establish, oppose, and control their own institutional life ranging from family to workplace, from gender to age.

Any dramatic art that aims to ally with cultural studies and cultural criticism and place contemporary theories in the foreground incorporates and insists on practices and strategies that deconstruct power relationships within the improvised or scripted performance stages. Once discerned, the dramatic elements provide insights and an arena for the participants, whether director or actors, playwrights, or audience, thus to demonstrate or intensely "feel" the power of human agency without force. In this case, the burden carried by dramatic artists is to position the participants in in-role activities and experiences that engage the political soul of the players. If able to rehearse through intelligence, initiative, and fantasy, and rehearse cultural hegemony that requires an initially nonhomogenous group, they will represent themselves as a social bloc with a solidarist collective will.

This is where Heathcote uses the concept of "Levels of Engagement." She claims that the dramatic process moves nonhomogeneously. If she can attract the individual to the dramatic session, she can engage their attention with a greater degree of groupness. From there, and through the intervention of dramatic strategies and tension, the teacher-in-role can build the collective will from attention to interest to concern to investment to commitment to obsession and then, maybe, a bit of learning. Throughout these levels of engagement, a complex structuring occurs, especially the students' in-role positioning, which moves from individualism to subject constructions (monks, archaeologists, detectives, or other symbolic collectives and from in-role positions), from role of mechanical labor to political authorities. "We" can make a difference and "We" can change the world is the collective voice of human agents (in-role) joined by hegemonic practices woven throughout the fabric of the ludic process of drama.

WAR OF POSITIONS

On one hand, it is uncomfortable at this point to introduce the metaphor of force and military violence—"war"—into a discussion on hegemony as consent without coercion. On the other hand, crucial to the discussion of hegemony is the importance of recognizing that hegemony is not fixed in space or time. Although hegemony mobilizes participants to reach consent, there is within that movement a "war of positions." In other words, there is within the consent a constant mediation, negotiation, and opposition to the multiple positions between two factions, and within a faction.

Femia (1981) refers to the war of positions as "a gradual shift in the balance of social and cultural forces" (p. 52). Unlike the "war of movement," which uses political combat and military confrontation and force, the war of positions uses "organic intellectuals" as the force that conquers the ideologies and wishes of one group that originally were dissimilar. In this way, the masses are integrated into the bourgeois, capitalist systems. As those systems and the agencies that engage hegemonic apparatuses become more and more articulated and ubiquitous, "What is needed is a 'war of position' on the cultural front . . . allowing the steady penetration and subversion of . . . the agencies of civil society (e.g., schools, universities, publishing houses, mass media, trade unions)" (p. 52). A war of positions can be arranged along a continuum allowing the introduction of an infinite range of strategies that highlight the opposing positioning of the dominant and the ruled.

For our purposes in the dramatic arts, the concept of a "war of positions" is perhaps the most important concept. Since the key element of a quality dramatic presentation or process is the building of tension, the positioning of issues and subjects in a dramatic context usually becomes "a choice between a violent or gradual and peaceful conquest of power" (Salamini, 1981, p. 131). When this arises in drama, Gramsci's concept of "war of positions" is useful. Without the holding power of dramatic tension, participants in the action move more into conflict that, again, is less a matter of tension and more a violent, militaristic, and coercive conflict. Students involved in a dramatic context that has built a "war of movement" usually yell at one another, or use physical violence, such as pushing and fistfighting. When a "war of positions" is built into the dramatic process or presentation, the moment is held in tension while the participants have to choose a position that everyone will consent to, or at least, form a solidly collective will.

Heathcote is a master of building tension using the concept "war of positions." With the employment of several dramatic conventions and her use of teacher-in-role and mantle-of-the-expert, Heathcote builds tension, not conflict, into the dramatic context. As the dramatic tension builds through hegemonic discourse and practices, the students who initially were opposing forces or complacent groups are placed in a position of having to choose both direction and method by which to reach a hegemonic state.

Since most of the information on hegemony is extensive, I found the least developed theme of Gramsci's theory was "war of positions." I feel this theme needs further expansion and has strong implications for dramatic activity.

RESISTANCES WITHIN HEGEMONY

Why talk of resistances when the topic of discussion is about hegemony (i.e., themes of the theory of consent). If, indeed, consent is what makes hegemonic moments, is there room within that process which encourages or allows resistance? Obviously, of course, there is!

Processes and practices of hegemony are not fixed or closed. In fact, it would seem that Gramsci would encourage the multiplicity and instability of hegemony through several concepts such as agency, subjective construction, historical contingency, and most recognizably through the resistances that exist in semiotic and political spaces. I feel that he offers hegemony as a concept from which "to act and to diffuse power with which to take advantage of the range of mobile and transitory points of resistance inherent in networks of power relations" (Lather, 1991, p. 39). Although there may be consent between the "war of positions," "no dominant culture ever in reality includes or exhausts all human practice, human energy, and human intentions" (Milner, 1994, p. 72). Thus, the lack of inclusiveness in reality transfers to the impossibility for a totality or closure in any grand narrative, including the theories of hegemony.

It seems that the major focus of contemporary theories is to challenge modern cultural constructions for the existence of exclusions, dominance, and power. Being positioned in the midst of multiple and contradictory discourses, institutions, and other cultural structures invites resistance even within the hegemonic moments of culture. Further alignment with contemporary theories places theories of resistance within the concept of hegemony. Both appeal to the empowerment of agency and subjectivity and act as a challenge to the "in-class" knowledge, truths, beliefs, behaviors, institutions, and so forth.

With hegemony comes counter-hegemony. Counter-hegemony functions to provide resistance, agency, and sources of cultural innovation required for the fundamental transformation of society. If hegemony is nonviolent, noncoercive, and a state of consent, it most definitely is never a state of consensus or complacency among the masses or the "war of positions." Hegemony is definitely a constant struggle for consent to positions of knowledge, gender, history, and so forth. Counter-hegemony works to share "the sense of political struggle, growing out of the intimate relations lived within an oppressed community, and the effects of those relations and on that community of a politics of resistance" (Miller, 1990, p. 129).

Within the dramatic arts context and processes, the participants build commitment, and tension is introduced into that commitment. Again, dramatic tension is the key element that produces states and recognition of power, oppression, privilege, and marginalization. Tension freezes the recognition in dramatic time and space to allow moments of self-reflexivity—a key to empowerment and human agency. Given the power to choose, the participants frozen within the time and space of the dramatic tension and confronted with the "war of positions" are faced with the possibility of counter-hegemonic imaginations. Trapped within the dramatic world of possibilities and offered sustained contestation and resistance, the participants challenge the power of the dominant group's knowledge, truth, gender, or whatever, and are authorized through dramatic agency to overcome the "war of positions" through counter-hegemonic practices. With strategies directed by contemporary theories at their disposal, dramatic artists embark on a journey of counter-hegemony and resistances kept afloat by the ludic imagination. And as Foucault claims: Since there is a plurality of powers, therefore, there is a plurality of resistances and he refuses to privilege one as any more revolutionary or universal than any other (Usher and Edwards, 1994).

HEGEMONY AS HISTORICAL CONSCIOUSNESS

The term "historical" is used here not as a subject of study with a specific content but as a force that constructs who we are and how we came to be. This includes any world making. In *The Uses and Abuses of History,* Nietzsche alerts us to the "illusions of truth" (Sarup, 1993, p. 90) that both color our past and present constitutions of subject and world and our thoughts and actions within. For example, one of the common phrases of the feminist and women's movements is about our stories—what do we keep and what do we throw away? To extend this further, we would ask what is knowable and what is unknown about our stories. Needless to say, women have been abused by the historical privileging of the male figure. In fairness, however, men have also been slotted to categories that have become stereotypical images of men and women, and impacts on relationships to self, other, and world.

At the same local high school mentioned in Chapter 1, the students were being taught Greek history by a very competent student teacher. He had a natural pedagogical sense of delivering history and, in this case, the Persian and Peloponnesian Wars. He was, however, missing a critical edge. As he talked about the wars and the social, cultural, political, and economic conditions from a textbook on this period of history, I was struck by the illusions of truth portrayed in the text and, more dangerously, in the minds of this teacher and his students. Although these students were engaged in the unfolding drama of Greek history through the stories of the student teacher, several points seemed to be missing. From the back of the room, I realized the discourse and viewpoint were about and by males. None of the young women in the class challenged the fact that the entire content of the lesson was distorting, devaluing, and neglectful of the role of women at this time. The students' discourse included Cimion, who, coming from a privileged family, was elected to the Greek council, and that coming from this wealthy family he was expected to "be like his dad." On this note, the students are now left with the impression that if women were to be valued, they needed to be like their mothers, or to be like their fathers. In either case, you can see and understand the abuse of history. Either the women were not part of, responsible for, or affected by the conditions of the time or what they were doing at the time. They were given no role in "his-story." What hegemonic practices were in place here that left the student teacher with a mono-gendered version of history and the women students consenting to history as constituted and privileging men in the "high stories" (etymology of "history") of the Greeks and others?

The main emphasis on the lesson was the rivalry that leads to war. The comment was "we shed a lot of blood." The quote was in reference to blood, blood, blood everywhere, shed by the men, egged on by the rivalry to go to war. The truth is that at no time were there any discussions of alternative routes that could be taken in order to prevent war. In this way, we continuously abuse our history and more importantly, for our purposes, abuse the teaching and learning of history.

I am using history here as the arena for the theater of historical consciousness that impacts upon the participants, in this case, a group of secondary school students. Theater can play a role in this reconstruction. Theater that is for or by children should be included in the arena of the history class. At no point, and this seems common to several types of lessons, were steps taken to "retrace" the history instead of "tracing" the history, but neither were there attempts to develop a "forking-paths" approach to history. On the other hand, theater by and for children should encourage if not demand that children, through any of dramatic arts strategies and conventions, reroute and reuse, but not just recycle historical consciousness.

To bring forward the role of women provides a critical image for scenarios and processes of historical knowledge. In addition, theater that reroutes history in a forking-path manner engages the students with the content not only in a cultural studies perspective but also a "possible worlds" scenario. If we took, for example, the previous example of the Greek wars, we could consider not how rivalry causes war (which is a very scientific cause-and-effect approach to any study) or leads to war, but how rivalry becomes the condition that leads to peace without war or violence (a possible hegemonic process). The danger here or the abuse of this strategy (and thus the abuse of history) is that we have no sense of what leads to war. This is without a doubt a fact of our lives and a dominant historical consciousness. The real abuse lies in the fact that through our study of history we do not consider the alternative routes or stories that should be told.

What if at the time there were living people who actually were using rivalry to lead to peace? We could rework our historical imagination, create a group or individual who is lifted off the pages of the history textbook, lifted out of the conceptual prison of the teacher's mind, out of the historical entrenched minds of the students, and put on stage as a group how rivalry leads to peace without war or violence (physical, emotional, psychological, etc.). If the alternatives are explored through the dramatic conventions, the boundless borders of our theatrical imagination could still use history in creating illusions of truth. The fact is that peaceful alternatives could mean complacency on the part of the weak or conquered, or still worse, the taking of slaves by the master/national country. Perhaps the group foregrounded could not only consist of women but children who take the forking paths in their creation of a theatrical work.

Unlike Rosencrantz and Guildenstern, who are dead and live between the lines and spaces of the Shakespearean text and see history from their point of view, rerouting of history through theater allows us to step into history and take different paths. This rehearsal of history making is a popular device in movies and television in which people are transported back and forward in time and given a chance to change the route of history. The writer, playwright, or director, however, still enter the time zone with their own perceptual and conceptual frameworks. At the point in which history could take one path or the other, they still would have to choose the path that leads to the historical event as we know it in the present day. In this type of theater, the idea would be to bring the audience or the participants to the point to which they can choose one path or the other.

Chris Jenks (1993), in his article on the "Necessity of Tradition in Cultural Reproduction," extends Nietzsche's discussion on the uses and abuses of history (p. 125). Baudrillard (1988) and Lyotard (1989) feel that a total break with history is the only way in which we will leap into postmodern worlds. This break with history is not a mere pronouncement of the end of society, but "an unprecedented fracture between the signs, symbols, rituals, images, knowledge, and narratives of past and present history" (Jenks, 1993, p. 131). Sociologists conventionally shy away from such thought; even the variety of perspectives in sociology do not seem to generate alternative realities but rather politicized versions of common sense. Social scientists are not properly socialized in the disciplined yet disruptive way of their tradition. We do not try hard enough to disrupt, invert, subvert, and destabilize everyday consciousness. Our practice becomes conservative and unable to theorize alternative realities, susceptible to the destabilizing complaints of, for example, the postmodern.

History is constantly held within the vicelike grip of construction instead of reconstruction. In other words, history does not construct its own problems; it has them provided. We begin an enfeeblement brought on by a nonflexible relation to tradition inflated through the influence of positivism and lack of historical imagination that reconstructs fact through fiction (dramatic arts). Truth is no longer an illusion of truth. When we subvert history, we resist it. When we begin to legitimize it, tradition is necessary. We need history to remind us not of who we are, but how we came to be. If we did not ignore the past but reconstructed it by excluded ghosts, resistance would not be to the historical reconstruction of the world through theatrical bending or blurring but to the corruption of historical thought and practices lodged positivistically and hegemonically in our consciousness.

As symbolic ordering, history places a continuity of experiences and cultural constructions that are legitimized by the present and by contemporary discursive organization—that is, hegemony. If the past, ideologically and hegemonically constructed in a modern society, is burdened with myths, legends, and stories as modern theories were once diagnosed to be so, then the case is similar for premodern society. Since the structures of history in modern society are seen as universal, timeless, or arbitrary segments of the human consciousness, the purpose of introducing deconstruction strategies and hegemonic awareness within a historical consciousness is to prevent the structuralist notion that cancels history. Even when applying a theory of consent, questions about history should not be about universals and privileged fragments of information but about change and innovation in cultural constructions over the historical epoch. As Benhabib (1992) asks, "Should we approach history to retrieve from it, the victims, memories, loss, struggles, and unsuccessful resistances, or should we approach history to retrieve from the monotonous succession of infinite 'power/knowledge' complexes that materially constitutes cells?" (p. 223). In choosing the latter route, implications about how we rethink and reclaim lost or misrepresented cultural constructions, such as gender and race, impose new alternatives to change the future.

Hegemonic apparatuses would problematize historical knowledge, and would resist "preferred" or "dominant" readings of history. In the modern world, history has been defined and constructed mainly by a bourgeois population that, for material purposes, would obviously privilege their history and selected discourse and images that in effect silence all other members who do not belong to the bourgeois class.

Perhaps groups that have submitted to the universalization of Western, European/American, white, middle-class, male, elite history have been those nations or races colonized by this elite. Williams and Williams (1993) discuss how Arabs and knowledgeable sensibilities have resented the racial doctrines of twentieth-century writers of history. They use the example of the book *The Seven Pillars of Wisdom* as an example of history as racial discrimination. Their thesis suggests that the prime mover of Arab unity was an Englishman (Lawrence of Arabia), which promotes the myth that a white, European male in a position of leadership is an essential ingredient if people of color are to pursue a national goal and be an effective fighting force. This reading relates directly to the tradition of hegemonic Western discourse. Historical content presented through any of the dramatic arts would need to be challenged especially by the theories of postcolonialism.

THEATER OF MEMORY

No other area of consciousness is affected as much as that of the construction of the world and our lives through history. The constitution of the subject and our world through the discourses, structures, and mythology of history has brought us to a point in the modern world that has narrowed notions of social reality. We become imprisoned in one system of thought as a zone of the familiar and the legitimate. For our purposes (drama as an agent of change and a shift or change in our historical consciousness), we need to challenge and question the change in terms of the dominant concepts and structures that have arrived on the doorstep at the end of the modern world. No longer welcome without challenge, historical consciousnesses are shifting and changing dramatically.

In this section, the historical consciousness is privileged only if it allows itself to be maneuvered, manipulated, and challenged through dramatic conventions and the theories of cultural studies. When the Theater of Memory (Fuentes, 1975) is applied to a theater/drama event and frosted with theories of cultural studies, historical memory is transformed. As the revisionists "demystify or debunk the orthodox version of the past" (McHale, 1989, p. 90), the strategies range from the displacement of officially accepted history to the insertion of lost or suppressed knowledge to crossing between the seams of historical facts, events, and eras. The dramatic arts as a means for the rehearsal of possible realities is not purely a case of futurist indulgences of science, fantasies, or afterworld thinking. In all seriousness, they are a consideration of the implications for critical thinking and the application of theories borrowed from several fields such as deconstruction, poststructuralism, and the philosophies of postmodernism.

What lies in store for a theater that is changing and reconstructing the historical consciousness and moves from the familiar structures of both traditional Western theater and Eastern theatrical traditions? As we experiment with the historical consciousness of the past, we divert and insert unfamiliar presences and facts as well as illegitimate, unjustified, acceptable norms of history. We explore the regions of the modern world as a present moment/decade/century/era—even in which we are presently immersed (or however we define modern times)—and finally exert some creative energy in presenting possibilities for the future.

As with any theoretical explorations into the pragmatic world of reality, and doing so through the illusionary world of drama, we could in the end remove all intent or possibility of a postmodern world that is indeed ideally full of justice and equality, and an acceptance of diversity as we hope—at least in theory. The global decadence of the modern age, the decline in the powers of Western society, the emerging dominance of Eastern cultures through capitalist markets and divisions provides a backdrop upon which any theory that claims to reconstruct a new world must be used with caution, hesitation, and skepticism. We must consider the exploration of the world through the dramatic arts merely as a playful means of helpful hints and serious configurations of possibility.

Any new thinking requires substance of practice, and whether playful or serious consequences, the governing elements such as drama, especially in a pedagogical, educational context, must be scrutinized for inhuman consequences. As Fuentes's (1975) *Terra Nostra* suggests in his Theater of Memory, "history repeats itself only because we are unaware of the alternate possibility for each historic event; what that even could have been, but was not. Knowing, we can ensure that history does not repeat itself; that the alternate possibility is the one that occurs for the first time" (p. 644).

The dramatic arts that consider reconstruction of the historical consciousness do not pretend that this is only a play world; they use the arena to throw up obstacles to the historical process. These obstacles such as memories of the past serve to illuminate not only what is but what could be. The question remains not so much an insertion or change of the historical consciousness but a problem of what to keep and what to throw away in our historical sensibilities. The legends, myths, and facts that sit on the porch of normalization and legitimization can be sorted through some to-be-discarded memories (assuming they oppress or devalue persons). The post–World War II youth must daily ask themselves the questions of what to keep and what to throw away about the events of World War II. Christa Wolf and other Jewish writers want to keep visible what is gradually disappearing from our historical consciousness in regard to the residue of guilt in postwar Germany. The dramatic context serves as a location for the ever-changing categories of identity based on the constructions from our historical consciousness.

Another literary device used by the deconstructionist and poststructuralist is that of erasure, mentioned in Chapter 2, in which thoughts and discourse can be crossed out of our consciousness. A fun technique on one hand, but not on the other, it is subject to the possibility of abuse. For example, Birringer (1991) talks about the squatter's movement. As the state bureaucrats demolished and remodeled war-torn buildings, not only did they displace the homeless but they removed the memories of war. Squatters who moved into the area were providing a "cultural, political resistance to the hegemonizing tendencies of the bureaucrats, and also reproduced exploitation and self oppression through guilt" (McHale, 1989, p. 16). Playing with the historical consciousness requires a historical break with the normalization and globalization of social and cultural relations.

Lyotard's (1989) request for a refusal of history as a postmodern break with the modern world is one of the inherent abuses of historical memory. In drama, whatever strategy or illusion is used to review and reshape the historical consciousness, we must always honor the subjects who were both the creators and the victims of the historical consciousness. We abuse the historical memory as much by the elimination or devaluing of groups, but even more so if we leave out the suffering, struggle, and pain of the victims throughout history. All traces of history and social relapse into the objective and rationale world of modern society has separated the subject from its history. The vulnerability of power and knowledge in a postmodern historical consciousness can become the unwelcomed guest at the trans-historical party. Our need to distrust history and locate dominance through the rehearsal world of drama can put brutal pressure on our theories and practices and even more dislocation of the underprivileged and dispossessed.

Whether through the theatrical discourse of text or stage presentation, all we wish to remember or understand yet reconstruct is our historical consciousness and traditions as a politics of representation that intellectually challenge and awaken us to both the dreams and the nightmares of history. Like Muller, who sees theater as a continuous recapturing of revolutionary memory, and Benjamin, who asks for dialectical images that flash the significant past as moments of extreme danger, the Theater of Memory recognizes the accumulative crises of an unchallenged, forgetful history. In summation, Willis (in Doyle, 1993) best expressed that it is necessary to investigate the forms of lived cultural productions in terms of what is inherited as well as what is imposed. To support this, Madeline Grumet (in Doyle, 1993, p. 46) is quoted as saying that "drama in schools must do more than fill in the spaces of traditional formulas, it must be willing to go beyond the predictable, and point to possibility." From this, each dramatic strategy or event that we plan or use must ask questions based on the historical consciousness that shows the contradictions of social reality (e.g., hegemony, symbolic violence) but again asks whose knowledge, values, behavior, history is being served, dominant, privileged and how can we create resistance to the dominance?

One of the most immediate threats to our rebellious interiority, claims Agger (1991), is a loss or entrapment of memory. In line with Nietzsche's uses and abuses of history is the hegemonic element of entrapped memories. Because such memories act as legitimation for the privileging of certain actions, entrapped memories themselves must be deconstructed, challenged, and resisted as pure, or as absolute knowledge and truth. The introduction of counter-memory intervenes in the historical consciousness. Counter-memory, claims Marshall (1992, p. 150), intervenes in history rather than chronicles history. Entrapped memories interrogated by counter-memories will not accept the past as privilege or truth.

POPULAR CULTURE AND HEGEMONY

The most influential, hegemonic apparatus that exists at the end of the modern century is popular culture, especially the media of television and film, and more recently, multimedia technology. Gramsci (1973) claims "that the culture industries reproduce capitalist hegemony over the working class by engineering consent to the existing society, thereby establishing a socio, psychological basis for social integration" (p. 131). Several dramatic arts have been influenced by the distribution of cultural representations produced by popular culture. In other words, representations of truth, knowledge, gender, race, and age are generated by the ubiquitous presence of popular culture.

> The concept of hegemony clarifies how cultural power is able to penetrate the terrain of daily life, transforming it into a struggle over, and accommodation to the culture of subordinate groups. Second, ... [popular culture is involved in] the production of subjectivity ... as a pedagogical process whose structuring principles are deeply political. And thirdly, popular culture ... serves in contradictory ways to empower and disempower various groups. (Giroux, 1992, p. 188)

The challenge is how popular culture mobilizes and ultimately puts into service specific political agendas. Culture leads politics (Grossberg, 1992, p. 255). By encoding text, popular culture implies and reproduces hegemonic ideologies and images of cultural constructions—the medium is the message.

HEGEMONY AS CONTINGENCY

If indeed hegemony is a process that is discursive and historical, what are the implications for the dramatic arts, especially the rehearsal process, or for the dramatic arts as an educational site through cultural studies and criticism? In terms of connecting hegemony and the dramatic arts, where is the line between exploitation of the human imagination and serious theoretical application to the dramatic arts? What becomes hegemonic about the dramatic arts when the participants, from actors to audience, are involved for entertainment instead of political and intellectual insights? What hegemonic apparatuses are being used to have the participants of the dramatic arts consent by coercion? force? dialectic? theoretical amorization? fluff? pedagogical charisma? entertainment? fun?

In the rehearsal process (assuming the professor/teacher/director/actors/students are aware and have identified their own hegemonic practices), the dramatic text can most easily be dismantled for several modern cultural constructions that are in crisis. Once identified, the project is to ask what discursive and historical processes occurred that brought the constructed textual elements to the moment of hegemony (i.e., moments that are fleeting). Hegemony itself is never fixed in space or time but subject to continuous positioning and repositioning, thinking that is consistent with contemporary theories.

In closing, I would like to draw the reader's attention to other metaphorical concepts of hegemony. Hegemony as seduction (Miller, 1990), as Orientalism (Said, 1978), and as other metaphors permits a plurality of discourses to surround the cultural constructions and encourages dismantling culture based on recognizable, relevant, and yet creative dismantling strategies.

CHAPTER 6

Acting against the Grain

THEORIES INTO DRAMATIC PRACTICE

The most important function of dramatic arts strategies that carries theories of cultural studies and criticism is to dismantle mainstream, status quo, modern, cultural constructions that are in crisis. Therefore, the following dramatic practices are directed at deconstructing representations of modern society to explore possibilities of rehearsing for a postcritical, postmodern, poststructural, postformal, and postcolonial world. Needless to say, there are loopholes within these areas. As the notion of ludic postmodernism suggests, the application of cultural studies theories seems to support the play and process orientation of the dramatic arts. The ludic yet serious and rigorous distancing of the dramatic arts provides a safe space to dismantle modern cultural constructions. At this point, the reader might be asking—So what? They have been saturated with contemporary theories, deconstructionism, and historical hegemony. So what are the connections and implications for the dramatic arts?

Throughout the text so far the main purpose of introducing students to contemporary theories has been to provide a framework that dismantles modern cultural constructions and modern consciousness in order to revamp, remodify, and, in essence, change aspects of our lives. At the moment, this may seem to be a daunting task. In any of the dramatic arts, whether it be mime, improvisation, clowning, or performances, the daily input of contemporary theories modifies or changes directions and structures.

With this in mind, the purpose of this chapter is to provide some strategical thinking that will help us rethink our dramatic practices through the influence of contemporary theories. Dramatic artists can use the contemporary theories in this book to inform their practices. The ludic persona allows the dramatic artist to engage contemporary theories in a playful, ludic manner with a sense of humor, parody, irony, and vigor. Similar to any work in the arts, sloppiness is not a credible or legitimized arena of curricula or drama. Therefore, a rigorous theoretical push to inform practice is necessary to maintain a respectable and respected attitude for the dramatic arts.

Finally, and more importantly, the dramatic artist must proceed with political commitment—in other words, with an attitude that all learning, curriculum, pedagogy, and theory employs political agendas to create new ways of thinking, new consciousness, new histories and rewritings. A final cautionary note: There may not be any fundamental essence to the dramatic arts, no fundamental strategies, but there is one foundation through which the dramatic arts filter. That is the ludic imagination—the willingness, power, attitude, resources, strategies, energy, and interest to live in the ludic imagination, the world of dramatic play. A final note to teachers, professors, and students in the dramatic arts: We must be willing to interrogate and dismantle modern cultural constructions and be unafraid to find out about ourselves and others. We must be willing to dismantle knowledge, values, and so forth that are taken for granted, mainstream, status quo, quite secure, familiar and known, or a threat. We must move into these deconstructed worlds that may find us too close to home, the past, family, or friends, that will shock, scare, or sicken. If we dare, we are pedagogical artists in the true sense.

QUESTIONS THAT DISMANTLE CULTURAL CONSTRUCTIONS

The main strategy that cultural critics use is the question! In Chapter 3, the priority of the question was introduced as the major element in the deconstruction of cultural texts. In this chapter, questioning is valued as a key element in the deconstruction and dismantling of the modern/cultural constructions. The kinds of questions formulated are important to a cultural studies way of knowing, learning, being, teaching, and acting—in the dramatic arts and in life. The following is a list of possible questions and conversations to ask before, during, or following a scenario.

The ideal way to employ them is to somehow move the director/teacher in-role, to circulate the questions within the "action" of the dramatic context, not outside the dramatic action. With any of these questions, definitely rework them but also include or create your own.

The following questions are taken from drama classes involved in cultural studies. They are a good source of questions to apply to dramatic arts with some modifications and changes related to the scenario. It is strongly suggested that each student take one set of questions and apply it to the dramatic context that is under study. These questions could be asked of any improvised scenario or script and the host of other texts available to dramatic artists and writers. In turn, these questions can generate further or related questions. Once the theoretical perspectives of the rest of this book are discussed and understood, students should be able to apply the questions with increasing ease (hopefully in-role) and challenge the cultural constructions that are presented in dramatic processes, rehersals, and performances.

1. Gender stereotyping: Gender is perhaps the strongest element of cultural studies or perhaps the most obvious. Take it further to race or sexuality, and how much power is taken away with each cultural construction? Deeper than that is whose truths, knowledge, history, representations are valued? How is gender stereotyping produced/circulated/exchanged/mediated? Work in institutions? What is identity politics? Politics of difference?

2. This is modern life in crisis—the "grand narratives" that move everyone into categories determined by a larger entity that is all powerful. How do we have policies that prevent exclusions? How do we intervene theoretically? What is produced/circulated/exchanged that keeps exclusion based on size and other differences alive? Who decides what's inappropriate behavior? truth? knowledge?

3. How did legislation/policies help and limit? What happened before unions? What powers lie in institutional structures that force hegemonic (unchallenged) practices?

4. Immigrants: What is their struggle? What does colonization do for immigrants? Natives? What differences are more valued than "fitting in"?

5. What's respect? Censorship? Hegemony? Resistance? Counter-hegemonic practices? Can we institute policies and legislation against harassment in schools? Other locations?

6. How does discourse categorize/exclude/include differences? Recognition for integration: How? What are the institutional/government/powers at work here?

7. No need to say how many Americans can't identify with Miss America, racially, physically. What is hegemonic about awards, pageants, or mass media? What institutions do these support? How is beauty commodified? Capitalized? Body as object?

8. Depressed economic situations: Who's positioned how? Discourse legitimizing/privileging what cultural constructs of family here? Who is in power? Who positions whom and where? How? Why is there hegemonic control over the poor? Poor is constructed how? What ways? By what institutions, from family to church to government to colonial to texts (like print, television, film)? Intervention by whom? Poor? Non-poor? Public? Private? Government industry?

9. How does monolinguism act as a hegemonic practice? Why resistance? How does it become the site for hegemony, resistance, and counter-hegemony?

10. Let's decenter from this Euro-Amerocentric position. How? What happens?

11. God constructed as male? How did it get to be this way? Deconstruct on race, sexuality, and other differences. How/why is this image dominant? How is it circulated and maintained? In all institutions (family, church, school, military, etc.)? Think of the discourse that positions "God" as male and dominant in cultural constructions. Who benefits? Who/what challenged this cultural construction? What makes it unquestioned?

12. Credit cards as a symbol of power: For whom? Why? Why hasn't it changed? How could it change? How did it get to be exclusive? Think of who it excludes. Where/why does it get started? What cycle of power is circulated? Talk about desires as a commodity. Ask why so many people take it for granted.

13. What are the totalizing discourses, especially ones that exclude? What are the dominant discourses in institutions that invest its own power? What are the fixed boundaries that exclude, marginalize, invest power for/in the few?

14. How are the dominant boundaries questioned? Resisted? Challenged? Crossed? Which world is this? What is to be done in it? Which of my selves is to do it? What is a world? What kinds of worlds are there? How are they constituted? How do they differ?

What happens when different kinds of worlds are placed in confrontation? What happens where boundaries between worlds are violated? What is the mode of existence of a text?

15. What is the mode of existence of the world's text projects? How is a projected world structured? Verifiable standards of truth: Verifiable by whom? By whose standards? To what ends are they to be put?

16. What are the dogmatic systems of thought that require questioning of authority? How can we know the past today? How can we problematize history? How did [a given historical phenomenon] enter the system entitled "history" and how has that system of historical writing acquired effective discursive power?

17. Who is free to choose? Who is beyond the law? Who is healed? Who is housed? Who speaks? Who is silenced? Who salutes longest? Who prays loudest? Who dies first? (Kellner et al., 1991)

18. Exclusion based on gender, physical difference: Think of the discourse of physical differences. How are they constructed in a way that positions people so they are represented as in power or as dependent or independent? How is physical difference a political issue? Throughout history, how has this been constructed?

19. Sites of desire as capital? What really gains power? Why is censorship a powerful force? Who benefits in terms of money/power by censorship? Why/how is it not challenged or resisted? How have gender/race/physical differences been created? Circulated? Why can this continue?

20. Forefathers? Discourse is language of power. Traditions are filled with exclusions also. So what history do we keep/throw away as oppressive, exclusive? Names/naming as exclusionary or as giving power? How did you know this history? Who/what was truth? Recorded/not recorded/not passed on about your/his/her history? Is it romantic? Why is English so privileged? Dominant? Whose truths? Who decides what is true/not true? How is power gained, maintained, circulated through language? How does language construct culture? Why are there no challenges to loss of language? Does a distinct society based on separation overcome language borders/margins?

21. The institution has power. How do they get it? How is it maintained? Why no resistance? Or what happens when we resist? The borders created by institutions such as marriage: Do men

still control women's bodies? How are single women represented through several cultural apparatuses such as medicine,
media, church, and so on?

22. Colonial discourse: Help the poor/homeless by diverting funding? Keep positioning people in powerless positions? Who are
the agencies of power? Powerlessness? How do the powerless/
poor/silenced/oppressed gain agency to resist/challenge/change
power systems institutions?

23. There are many versions/theories/positions and positioning
of/about women. There is backlash, which sounds like part of
your scenario. Solidarity is a political act, a power act. Sisterhood gains power how? Why? Consider the history. When we
subject/are subjects of theory/perspectives/grand narratives, we
"lump" everyone. What is valued about/for/by women? Who
stays/creates/circulates/dominates certain representations over
others? Who speaks for whom? Why? How?

24. "Roles" are borders. How does popular culture represent
"roles"? Why? What language (discourse) positions us? Sports
are constructed along certain systems of class/race/gender/phys-
icality/mentality/privilege, and so on.

25. What language is dominant? (What's the history of who's been
in power for centuries?) Even with bilingualism who's still excluded?

26. Parents in the school: What institutional structure and policies
exclude? Why do or don't parents intervene?

27. Why do systematic power structures start to be dependent
on pornography? On censorship? Big issue: How does it position men, women? How does pornography get started/
produced? What issues arise of freedom/of individual and social
control?

28. Cultural constructions from family, church, law, medicine,
ethics, value: Unpack the systematic exclusions? Silences?

29. How the discourse and so on construct this culture and how it
has worked for and against the voiceless.

30. Computers: A crisis in modern life? How do they (and all
connected) have power over us/the modern world? Crisis of
knowledge? Value? Gender/race/class/national and international?
Power: Who gets it? Circulates it? The seductive force of power?

31. Date rape: Look at the discourse that constructs it. How do we
educate, change, dismantle violent systems?

32. Body as object: Site of beauty, violence, birth, and exclusion? Power? Discourse?

33. Is a text to look at power? Exclusions? Values? Representations? Values? Who controls? Gender/class/age constructions?

34. How do churches/religions seduce/conform/exclude differences? Create dependency? Look at discourse of missionary work as power/master slave/relationship. Master/slave discourse: How circulated? How controlled? How resisted?

35. What is nationalism? What is lost/destroyed/eliminated by colonialism. How does cultural studies create questions that reclaim voices/land/culture/education/knowledge/values and so on? What powers prevent reclaiming? How?

36. Look at discourse of violence. Look at its history: How does it give power to certain groups/discourses and divert from production/roots of violence? What are the politics here?

37. But who still decides on criteria? Who benefits? Who is excluded? For jobs? For sports? Exclusions based on gender, age, education, class, money, heroes, legends, mythologies in Western culture.

38. Equity—pros/cons—talk of power/history/who should change? Gender/race/institutions?

39. Differently abled. How are they positioned in modern life? How does discourse position them?

40. Grand narrative that dominates, controls, site-specific to North America, discourse, how positioned family, friend, school, media. Whose codes? How encoded? Resistance? Misbehaving against what? Who? How? Resistance? Hegemonic? Why counter-hegemonic age? Gender, class, race, and so on.

41. Soup kitchens/food banks: Positioning? Institutional dominance? Identity politics? Identity crisis? Oppression/marginalizing? Why/how? Lack of agency for whom? Why? Representations? History? Colonization? Postmodern world: How do the marginalized get there? Move to the center?

42. What are the implications for deconstruction with multiple readings/texts/positioning/discourses?

43. Why does it work? Hegemony? What's a sense of humor and irony and/or sarcasm?

44. Discourse where it "slips" into oppressive use: This is called "troping," where we take meanings of discourse and let it slip into everyday/unchallenged use. Lissa Paul gave the example of

"I'm having a blond day" or another example is "I was jewed down to forty dollars." Challenge the constructs from a cultural criticism theoretical position. Ask cultural criticism questions.

45. We talk of sites of power and domination and the family is a major source along with hegemonic practices. What about outside home? What happens when the constructs that defined traditional women are gone? Are not part of the construct? Children, husband, men, marriage? Where's the power?

46. Why did women at one time (and still?) enter teaching and nursing? How do women's roles fit home, teaching, and nursing? Why are secondary teachers still mainly men, with fewer in elementary and almost none in kindergarten?

47. What is valued? Do men, women, race, sexual orientation construct home, relationships, teaching, nursing differently? How? Today, both teaching and nursing faculties are dominated in numbers by women. Why? Why hegemonic?

48. The power dynamics of discussion in the classroom. The right of individual expression/having something important to say over the right of social expression, everyone having something of value to say/to challenge. What other dominations and privileges occur because of gender, race, knowledge, truths, history, language, or oppression of speech? Not just obvious constructs but sometimes constructs put forth by popular culture and legitimized by them? Who legitimizes conversations/discussions? Who's legitimized by popular culture? Media? How? How sustained?

49. An excellent text or folktale: Who selects the constructs? From what position? What are the cultural constructs in fairy tales that are dominant, privilege certain subject constructions over others?

50. Who constructs nationalism? Who tells us a country is the most respected world peacekeepers? What about capital? Military colonialism? Military presence instead of independence for the occupied country? Who constructs? What constructs are in "peacekeeping" that take "agency" away from the occupied country? Who produced "nationalism" as a cultural/political construct? What is its history? What makes it work/not work/hegemonic? What are borders? How are they maintained? Collapsed?

51. Why is homosexuality a political issue? By whom/for whom has homosexuality been constructed? Why is it a threat? What are counter-hegemonic practices based on sexual orientation? How

are homosexuals excluded? Who and how is homophobia constructed? To whose benefit? Why?

52. Even advertisements are constructed to seduce us with buying
a product, and they are constructed to attract subjectivities.
How?

53. There is no fixed meaning or closure in poststructuralism and
deconstruction and our attempt to name concrete aspects of discrimination and prejudice. We are informed by certain truths and
knowledge (see Chapter 1) that already have us discriminate and
prejudged. These are very tied to crisis in modern thought and
discourse. Plus we are all positioned to interpret the cultural representations by our history, culture; objectivity is even "informed" by a dominant theory, as is our subjectivity. Now check
and revisit your comments to see what (who, when, why) has informed your knowledge and position.

54. The example used was very specific and concrete but mixed with
theory of culture studies, the politics of difference based on gender, boys excluding girls in soccer. Take the example further by
asking who gets to define the "rules," what is privileged in soccer? Brute force, speed, boys' bodies/girls' bodies? How did it
get like this? What are the images of what makes "good" soccer
games and players? Was your attempt to disrupt the power successful? Have boys discuss—except who still retains power and
authority? How does this position the boy? The girls? In relation
to power and authority? What if the rules said no soccer unless
50 percent girls/boys on a team? What about an assembly? How
would women discuss their own history of exclusion in sports?
Issue of money? Girls decide rules in collaboration with boys?
Trace the hegemonic apparatuses in place that create, circulate,
and maintain desire through sports.

55. Wheelchair accessibility? What denies people access to space,
time, others, knowledge, truth, power? Privilege? Body? Mind?
Soul? Money? What (who, how) is denied access through language? If you call me physically different, crippled, handicapped, differently abled, not able-bodied, how does that
position you and me? What can we do to dismantle the discourse
of inaccessibility?

56. Christmas concerts and other religions: First of all schools are
supposed to be state-run, separate from "church" law. But think
of the history of schools. Who started? Whose law? What is
dominant in schools? Parents? Who benefits? Think of this type

of exclusion in school history. Why? Think of current religious cleansing and integrated schools. Where does it start?

57. Car and mechanics: "Dear" is a discourse that is gender- and age- and power-structured. Mechanical jargon: Discourse is both expertise and "technical." Can they communicate in narrative? Other estimates (opinions, voices): Do we do that for other occupations? Resistances? Medicine, teaching, and so on? Not maybe unknowingly, but are there men who are unknowing about mechanics also? How have men been constructed that values them only for certain abilities? Did age/race/class/physical appearance/and so on come into play?

58. You did start to get at the cultural construction of race here. How is crime reported? Where is the store located in relation to class/race? How did it come to be that way? Why doesn't the store owner go elsewhere? Who are his "paying" customers? What is memory? Why are men the major population in prison? What is counter-memory? Why also certain races in prison? Now develop a policy for that neighborhood and the store manager that will change the power in privilege of one race over another. Also start to think identity politics. Prison systems as historically constructed: Read Foucault's information about prisons. What are entrapped memories inside/outside prisons? What memories oppress? Liberate?

59. A good start here might be both poststructuralism and postcolonialism theories. Do the latter think of why China might have to take these measures in population? What would you/we as Western European/North Americans do about the same "crisis"? Think of other solutions, policies. Remember our government at one time sterilized young native women as population control without their knowledge or permission. Read Germaine Greer's *Politics of Fertility*. How does adoption position China in relation to North Americans? If you were in China and Chinese what would you do? Where would you start? Think of Mao Tse-tung and his policies of the 1930s/1940s/1950s/Red Army. See both sides. Also consider media reports. Who selects the facts? How is China constructed by Westerners through media? Press? Literature? How would you (we) construct it from this? What cultural constructions are dominant? Think power and privilege. Think of what the colonization of China did. Does. Is doing. Future?

60. Changes are occurring. Think of race and class also and other cultural constructions and identity politics. Also how "jobs"—waitressing and so on—are constructed by males. Think of how males are "forced" into positions based on their jobs and how choices (gender) exclude and include them/us also. Also consider double/triple jeopardy. Exclusions based on more than one difference from mainstream. What policies and pamphlets would you develop to change or celebrate change?

61. What are possible actings of this scenario? How are actors in-role positioned? How are readings of character constructed? How are particular readings of subjects marginalized or privileged? How are cultural issues of race, gender, class, or religion produced by different acting of texts? What attitudes and values appear to be endorsed or challenged by different acting? What are possible endings for this scenario? How do these alternatives shift possible presentation of the scenario?

62. Clothing stores: A great text/site location for deconstructing size. Is it a construct, is it comparative? Competitive? Standardized? Your questions are great about who/how does fashion/size get decided on and the image/value that goes with it. Who decides "norm"? Why does the fashion industry go unchallenged (hegemony)? How/why does each of us contribute? Policy? Own clothing or cottage industries like Places in Africa (store in Chester, Nova Scotia), a cottage industry where African (privileges women) have co-op? What has big/mass technology done for women? Who are power names in fashion industry? Great questions and thoughts on your own questions.

63. What happened to physically/mentally different individual/groups before special education? What good has special education done/not done? What about naming/categorizing people? Discourse that excludes? Includes? Accesses? How are they empowered/not empowered? What is mainstream (according to gender, race, age, class, etc.)? Why is it that a person in a wheelchair has a "problem"? Do people not in wheelchairs not have problems? How are you/we positioned when we say "others" have a problem? How can we speak for others of different gender, race, and so on?

64. No female pitchers. The game of baseball is constructed by males (at one time only Caucasian); therefore abilities and differences of women would not be valued. Who is going to franchise a team

where a member is absent for nine months? The history of sports (as we in the Western culture know) goes back to Greek times when it was being constructed even then as a male cultural activity? Have to make women's sports valued/women valued? However, what about how "elitist" sports exclude? A modern crisis is a big one. See Reebok station on sportswomen. There are still major exclusions. What females do make it? What is hegemonic? Documentaries? What makes sports a symbol of the end of modernism?

65. Dolled up: Why a "doll"? Think of object—toy. Self-improvement defined as appearance! Social constructs of manners (whose? why theirs?): What's the history to this? Actually what beauty originally meant has nothing to do with physical alone—it is totally—that artistically talks about "moving to a state of grace and internal coherence." Somehow it's been misconstrued in modern times. What has produced/circulated "beauty" as we are bombarded by it today? *Baywatch:* produces "beauties" and circulates an image. Are there any race-different women on *Baywatch*? Think of the seduction and desire set in the minds of people who need to be saved. How popular culture is now determined rescue but best/only by a *"Baywatch* 'Babe' or 'Hunk' "? Challenge? How are behind the camera's eye shots selected? By whom? Maybe brains and beauty go together? What about caring? Inclusiveness as beauty.

66. Women's university, socializing, sister Claire. Maybe without saying the "f" word (feminism) you have the qualities, knowledge, challenge: Maybe I'm defensive here about my experience but at one time (15–20 years ago), my friends/myself wouldn't have been asking the questions you are asking? Maybe the two women have a knowledge/history that is important to education. Great questions especially about history in high school/university. A lot of cultural construction to challenge and deconstruct. Potential for video for secondary school.

67. Homophobia: Who constructed sexual orientation? Love, family, school, church, benefits, romance? Relationships are all cultural institutions constructed by heterosexual realities? Excludes many but largely homosexuals? Homosexual people were celebrated? When did it go "into the closet"? Why? By whom? What (whose) interests does it serve today? How do heterosexuals position themselves when they speak homophobia? Who gets to speak? Why? How?

68. Allergies? Who gets to control environment? How can allergy-prone people empower themselves? How do people become agents of change?

69. Males, white, European are paranoid right now, but everyone is. Afro-American males are paranoid; they fill the prisons, so imagine how they're excluded from legal rights. Women of color are saying feminism has been defined by white, academic, middle-class, so are they paranoid? There is a history: For centuries, women were excluded; they are 51% of population but not 51% in positions of power outside the home, so they are probably trying to balance 51% with positions still dominated by males—then race, then age—inclusiveness is a struggle but nevertheless a struggle, a political struggle. Neither you nor I is personally responsible for the way things are, but we are responsible for changing it. I would love to include physically different women in mainstream life and access empowerment for them. How do I resist their exclusion and create inclusion/power for them? Possible documentaries taking shape?

70. Tradition: It is filled with exclusions. How/who establishes traditions? How/why are they created? How are they maintained? Legitimized? Valued? What happens when challenged? How does discourse establish power in tradition? Why is tradition left unchallenged? Hegemonic practices?

71. Sisterhood clubs—lots of great advances for women. When the quality of life is raised for women, quality of life goes up/is raised for everyone—children/men/race/and so on. Sisterhood clubs like brotherhood clubs have a focus—sports, social, charity, women, and so on. If in the postmodern world these are eliminated because of discrimination, will there be blurring of boundaries between cultural groups? Then how do excluded groups/individuals get/obtain/keep political power?

72. Eve-teasing: Does it come from Garden of Eden that constructs Man–Woman–seduction but not harassment? Race? What education can take place in elementary/high school that would eliminate Eve-teasing? It happens in cities' crowded subways and I dare not inflict—he's usually bigger and stronger? How do we challenge/resist? What hegemonic practices are here? How/why is Eve-teasing produced/circulated/legitimized? What policies? The kinds to use are constructed by whom/how/why?

73. Old is not valued, costs money to maintain; not productive, therefore not valued. Relationships of seniors have been constructed. How/why? Where is the resistance? Popular culture? Youth is constructed in opposition to older categories? Who is privileged? How did it get to be this way? Always so? History of aging? Possible documentaries taking shape?

74. Popular fiction or "pulp fiction" is a source of deconstruction. How are men/women/race/sexual orientation and other exclusions based on differences constructed? How are they positioned as powerful/powerless/empowered? John Grisham does include women, but how? Sports is an extremely significant site/text for cultural studies interventions in the domination by males/race/ sexual orientation/physical/mental, and so on. Special Olympics? Country/western songs—another great site for exclusions. Poor k. d. lang—she was kicked out of Nashville—I wonder why? What is Reba McIntyre trying to do? Resist? Challenge? Are there others? Are men changing lyrics? Why? Money? Documentary?

75. Golf clubs have a history of exclusions: Gender, race, class, religion, sports are a vital text for cultural studies to deconstruct for power/resistance/discourse/modernism, and so on. Money is power, but for buying what? Consuming? Medical, education, legal (O.J.), housing—yes Madonna—we are a "material" people. Does money buy quality—yes—but of what? Baseball players? Documentary?

76. Why do women want commitment? Power here—why/what/ history? How to change? When do men/women commit to one another? History? How has the institution of dating/commitment/marriage been constructed along gender/race/age/family/ church/state/children/education/protection/success lines, and so on? A major site for cultural studies? Age is another rich source for cultural studies.

77. Sports are a major site for cultural studies theories and practices to be applied. Sports, besides being exclusive in gender especially, are also class exclusive and getting more so. Then O.J. becomes elitist and what happens? How do we resist/challenge elitism (based on gender/race/class/physical difference, and so on)? Cheerleaders: Do they get paid as much? Maybe cheerleading could construct their world differently? Still people cheering on men? Are there cheerleaders for women's sports?

78. Linguistic borders: This is perhaps the most major area of exclusion? How does it dominate/control/limit/change? How does language carry meaning/power (discourse)? How do claims of linguistic superiority serve groups? "Speak properly"—what does this mean? Discourse is a cultural construction. How did the secretary construct these people? How is she informed? What is the history that informed her? Whose? How do we change all this exclusion? Just appeals? Places to go for appeals? Many individuals/groups are threatened by backlash, by hegemony? How can we create counter-hegemony?

79. Classroom is a cultural construction where power and exclusion play themselves out. Once you are informed by certain theory (cultural studies), then you can see events, relationships, and so on, and go deeper to truths, knowledge that is valued/excluded, and so on, in the classroom. Now you have observed the surface. Go deeper to the truths. Whose is valued? Included? Science? Men's? Women's? European? Asian? What borders? How have they been crossed historically? Hegemonically? United States/Canada?

80. Physical appearance. Height is a measure of power or intelligence. Yes, it seems to be a measure of something other than physical, too. Where does the valuing of height come from? What is it an image of? Who/what produces/circulates/maintains height as power/valued? The classroom is a place of exclusion in discussions (large and small group)/lessons/textbooks. What happens in family/church/popular culture/sports/arts, and other major institutions that create borders and margins? Why does hegemony continue? Giants and dwarfs: In fiction/reality? What happens? Mainstream resistance?

81. Both men and women have been constructed about how/when to participate in discussion. It still continues even at university in meeting with my colleagues. More women are participating, but even some of them are not generous with their time/year. Why does this continue? What strategies (policies) will change this? Where does this model come from? What about race/class also?

82. Even the dramatic arts have gone bourgeois, defined by Broadway/London stage as valued (money). Where is the "fringe" theater in Toronto, New York, London, the margins? Do the homeless, the street kids, and so on go to *Phantom*? Is it a drama? The hegemony of it? The seductive aspect of Webber's

theater. Even Stratford has to do a musical every year to stay alive. Language has meaning/discourse is power—naming/ names are power or exclusionary. I never thought of red/yellow—now it's Asian American, etc. (In England, Native Americans are still called "Red Indians"—the colonizers have not changed. They still have Native Americans in a position?) Also, what's different about naming by race rather than by nationalities? Exclusions? What about colonial power to name? What question does postcolonialism ask about race? Nationality?

83. The church is an institution. It is and has been a major constructor of culture and has been (still) is exclusionary. Countries (race) at one time were organized by/bordered by the church. Who was dominant? What exclusionary practices did they enact/preach? All religions? Why? Why don't people speak out (hegemony) and challenge the dogma—the words? What is seductive? What happens when counter-hegemonic practices exist? Who makes policy? The classroom is a microcosm of larger structures of exclusion. How do classroom/education structures exclude? What do they exclude based on age/class/sexual orientation/race/gender/truth/knowledge/how we learn?

84. Marriage/relationships/gender relations are an institutional structure and have been embedded with culture constructions decided upon by gender/race/class/sexual orientation/physical/mental/ by parents/church/state/peers/media/literature. What truth/knowledge/history is at play here? Why? Who/what challenges the traditional, the familiar? How do capitalism/socialism organize/structure marriage in culture? Who is in power? Benefits?

85. Classrooms are a hotbed of exclusion. It goes deeper, to the way we've been taught. Boys and girls are socially constructed (theory). Watch for challenges to this and what happens if we accept our past, that is, use and abuse of history/tradition. See *Like Water for Chocolate* (movie).

86. Is the catalog—a popular source of fashion representations— changing values? Representations? But are they also a source (site) of power, privilege, and exclusion? To whom are they appealing? Seductive? Why did no one challenge them until recently? Even designs of clothing are exclusionary? What about buttons, zippers, and so on, for the physically different? Age different? How does mass consumerism exclude? Gain power? Seduce consumers? Who is privileged in buying? What cultural

constructions are there? Think of makeup/cosmetics in stores. Who are they directed at (based on differences of gender/ age/class/race/physically different and so on)?

87. Media is a great site to study cultural (popular culture) constructions of modern life (what technology makes available to the masses). Who/how do we challenge the images/representations? Why do we practice hegemony? How can we practice counter-hegemony against popular culture? How does it impact on uninformed consciousness? How is it used as power and privilege? Who benefits? What about Westernization of the world?

88. Talk about assimilation as a modern phenomenon in crisis, as a colonization of land, culture, truth, gender, race, and so on. The Middle East is a geographic, historic, and cultural construction by the West. How is it positioned in relation to "The West"? Read anything by Edward Said, Spivak, Gates, Wilson Harris, and others to see how domination of the "West" has constructed the "Other," especially the East and Caribbean, for the benefit of not understanding.

89. The other reason gender values/knowledge/exclusion/dominance come into the classroom is based on history of institutional structuring, by cultural power, norms, expectations, socialization. Read Patti Lather's *Getting Smart* (1991). How did she try to introduce feminist pedagogy in the classroom? Resistances? How? What strategies can you borrow here? If women had structured the classroom based on our construction, experience, ways of knowing/values/our knowledge, what would a classroom be like? What would other institutions be like if women constructed them? Physically handicapped–constructed institutions? If women's knowledge, truths, history were valued for themselves, what would the classroom be like? How does it change? How do we practice counter-hegemony?

90. Our constructions of time/space/relations/work/play are all cultural constructions structured to value some groups over others based on gender, race, class, physicality, and so on. You challenged the construction/the power/the exclusion/the ignorance. What are the consequences? How do you/we practice counter-hegemonic practices? What would a union do to worsen/better the incident? Who gets punished? Rewarded? How?

91. Relationships are a cultural construction. I bet when most people talk "significant other" they are talking about "opposite sex" other. Are these the only "significant others"? Look around you:

How many texts are constructed to privilege opposite sex relations, and how are texts constructed that makes us "desire" a significant other? Think of family, church, school, advertising, clothes, and so on. How does what is constructed make "significant other" a commodity?

92. United Nations has many aspects, peacekeeping one, but still military. Also Canada uses the United Nations (UN), like many countries, for money. It is also big business, big industry. So we can read the text from many positions. Success is a cultural construction also. Who gets to define success? Why are pieces of papers, certain jobs, certain activities constructed as successful? How do some get celebrity status, others not? (O.J. was successful!) What policies could be instituted? What resistances can be offered that would dismantle success as a commodified measure of a person?

93. Music is a very dominant cultural construction. It provides good cultural studies questions that deconstruct. Music is a commodity. High culture/popular culture: Who do they include/exclude? How some videos verge/or are pornographic/art? Think of Rita McNeill's (weight/harelip) exclusion from Jays' game? Who did they get instead? Who determines beauty? How does music industry/big business play on "desire"? They use cliched cultural constructions.

94. The O.J. trial as text is embedded with many subtexts and cultural constructions—multiple meanings/beginnings/endings and so on. Remember the families, Brown/Goldman. The Simpsons were also part of the "drug" culture? Why wasn't it brought out? Oprah Winfrey is a great text to bring in. She is seen as "an authority." She is quoted perhaps more than anyone as "an authority" on so many things. What a text to use! The subtexts of O.J.'s trial were presented in court so as to dismantle the "proof of experts." Furhman was used to establish "reasonable doubt"! And it worked. What is the task of lawyers (defense or prosecution)? What are ethics? Knowledge circulated and legitimized about law? Justice? Responsibility? Reporting? Media?

95. Science/arts: At one time, there was no split between disciplines. Where will postmodernism take us on this? Great questions on truth/knowledge. Be quite informed in cultural studies questions and exclusionary practices, not just on gender, race, class, and so on, but history, truth, knowledge. The dominance and privileges

given to some disciplines over others. How does it get to be so? Who legitimizes this? How? How can we dismantle this and make disciplines inclusionary of others' truths, and so on? What about cross-bordering disciplines? What does this mean?

96. Taken from Lather (1991, pp. 24, 113). Is Marxism too reluctant to accept dispersion and fragmentation to be useful? Is its ideal of a global, totalizing prospect of emancipation some new historical bloc, some new counter-hegemonic alliance, some new Archimedean standpoint too intrinsic to be done away with and still have Marxism? Is it too irredeemably structuralist, too tied to a premise that adequate knowledge grasps underlying structures and totalities of reality, a reality and a reason conceptualized as amendable to such understanding? At what point does the constant revision of the explanatory and predictive claims of classical Marxism exhaust it, creating a situation where Marxism no longer speaks to contemporary times? How do we address questions of narrative authority raised by poststucturalism in our empirical work? How do we *frame* meaning possibilities rather than *close* them in working with empirical data? How do we create multivoiced, multicentered texts from such data? How do we deconstruct the ways our own desires as emancipatory inquirers shape the texts we create? Why do we do our research? To use our privileges as academics to give voice to what Foucault terms "subjugated knowledges"? As another version of writing the self? What are the race, class, and gender relations that produce the research itself?

97. Taken from Femia (1981, p. 6). What, if any, are the underlying conditions for the emergence of a new culture, a new mode of thought and being? To what extent was Gramsci a voluntarist? What role did he assign to the economic infrastructure?

98. Taken from Grosssberg (1992, p. 259). How are cultural practices deployed into hegemonic struggles? How can popular culture be a strategic weapon in, as well as the ground of, hegemonic struggles? How can the reconfiguration of cultural spaces, places, and tempos itself become a principle of the rearticulation of structures of power? How are the dominant structures of power constituted and put into place?

99. Taken from Gamble (1988, p. 26). On the politics of support: At every blank, fill in a person, political party, and so on. How popular is _____? Who votes for _____? Has the _____ government

succeeded in overcoming so much internal and external opposition? Which classes and groups does _____ represent? How has
_____ been shaped by the doctrines of the New Right? The Left?
What is the relationship of _____ to _____? How is relationship
created? Circulated? Maintained? What tensions exist in the doctrine of the free economy and the strong state? On the politics of
power: Does the _____ government possess a viable accumulation strategy capable of reversing [a nation's] decline? How far
has the _____ government centralized the _____ state and in-
creased its repressive ways? Has the _____ government restruc-
tured the state? How radical were the policies of the _____
government and how successful has the government been in im-
plementing them?

100. Taken from Barker (1993, p. 109). Which history are we talking
about? What is the conceptualization of history in play? What is
its conception of temporal dispersal, teleological patterning, se-
quential and structural components and determinations? What
forces are admitted to be part of it, what are its dimensions, what
lies outside it? Whose history is it? What political and ideological purposes does it formulate and serve? What is its gender?
Race? Nationality? Class?

101. Taken from Miller (1990). Why, and how, are women seduced
by men, and how do they live with and resist that seduction?

102. Tell us about someone you know (in your family, on your street,
from your past, a friend, in your community) who has been excluded? If you were the writer of this scenario, where and how
would you have gotten your ideas and notions about the characters, the setting, plot, experiences, knowledge, gender, race, age,
physical being? Tell us how events or people in this scenario
have or have not changed your life. Tell us about people, places,
events, scenes that you have known or seen that are similar or
different from peoples, places, events, and so on that are in your
book. Talk about what went through your mind as you were acting in this scenario. Make yourself or someone you know a hero
or villain in this scenario. Why? How? Tell us what the actors
made important to you? Why? Tell us if there is anything that
has happened to you or someone you know that is similar or different to that in the scenario. Tell us what ideas the actors gave
you? For change? To find discourse that is similar to you? Would
you use or not use it in some way in life? Why or why not? Tell

us about words you would use or not use to describe people you know, events, or experiences that are part of your life in some way. Find discourse you would use (or a friend, or others you know) or have heard others use that would change this scenario for more inclusion?

103. Are there any subjects/subject constructions you want to challenge? Were there conflicts that the actors included or did not include in the story? Contradictions? Have you had experiences similar to the actors in-role? Go in-role and introduce the experience. Do you remember thinking about your experiences? Tell us about people, places, events, and scenes that you have known or seen that are similar to those in this scenario. Tell us what the actors made important for people? Age? Gender? Relationships? Institutions? History? Local knowledge?

104. Tell us about events or people in this scenario that have or have not changed today. Expose the existing power structures in this scenario. Go in-role as a reporter or media representative to do so. Are there characters who seem to have more power than others? Why? How? How do the actors reveal subjectivities, descriptions, dialogue, behavior, other characters' reactions or lack of them to him or her? Where have these power structures been built into the construction of the institution of this scenario?

105. Are stereotypes or discriminations inherent in this scenario? What subjects have or do not have "voices"? How? Why? Which representations are realistic? Not realistic? Whose values are reaffirmed or questioned? How? By whom? Why? How do values and attitudes fit in? Change? Oppress?

106. What and how may attitudes, opinions, and expectations limit people, as in this scenario, from trying new things? From being valued? Centered? Included? Does it seem that the subject is forced/pressured to act or think in certain ways? Does she or he have a voice? Or not? Why? How is she or he silenced in any way? What characters have power in this scenario? Why? How?

107. What attitudes, opinions, and beliefs do we bring to the reading of this dramatic text? Do we value older people's opinions and beliefs? Do you know someone that reminds you of any of the subjects? Actions?

108. Who and where are the people who "do or do not exist" in this scenario? Who has a voice and/or who does not? Who is presented but downgraded? Tell us about some experiences or situations you

have had or been in where someone trivialized or dismissed your point of view. Introduce reasons why people may formulate attitudes/opinions about others that are demeaning, discriminating, or stereotyping.

109. How and what is the position of the subject by the way the scenario was performed? Challenge some of the beliefs. Your beliefs? What are some of the social constrictions/demands placed on people in this scenario? How is this done? What desires do the subjects have? Why? What cultural artifacts constructed the subject's desires?

110. What options to challenge, or change, were or were not open to the subjects? Deconstruct some of the comments, cliches, and tropes made by the subjects toward one another or other subject constructions.

111. What historical constructions are represented in this scenario? Is it different than the traditional structures? How? Why? Is there anyone who is left out or treated unfairly in the scenario? Who? Why? How? What attitudes or values appear to be endorsed in this dramatic text? Who is in power in this scenario? Is this fair and just? Does one gender dominate another in this text? How? How not? Why? Do you know someone who lives alone like the actor? What is the traditional opinion of a young woman/others that live alone? How does that marginalize single women/them? Would you or do you know someone who would feel excluded or marginalized by this reading of the status quo, norm, mainstream? Why do you think the daughter came to live with her father when she had a baby? Were there social or economic reasons that might have forced her to do so? Would it have been a different situation if the old man's son brought his baby home to stay with her grandfather? Why? What is the traditional stereotype about single parents? Do you know someone who is a single parent? How are they like the mother in the scenario? What statement do you think is being made about single parenthood?

112. What cultural constructions are violent? How are constitutional structures (family, work, church) violent? How? Why? Do you know someone who has a life that is far from peaceful, that is, violent or warlike and so on? Why does it seem that peace is not easily attained? How does this apply to the person whose life is filled with violence?

113. Do you know someone who is elderly and lives alone? How is their life like a grandparent's? How did the scenario portray the

elderly and their way of life? Do you think this is a true and equal representation of the issues facing the aged? What is the scenario saying about old age? Is this in line with conventional thinking about the abilities of the elderly?

114. What does this scenario say about God and Heaven? Dominant religions? Retell the story from the position of someone who has different beliefs/religion.

115. Who is in power in this story? How does it change? What statement does this story make about power and who should and should not have it? How are subjects "troped"? What is exclusive? Privileged?

116. Do you know someone who is bigger and/or stronger than you who has treated you unfairly because of your size, age, gender, and so on? How did they address you? The subject? Conventions? Discourse? How does this change the power relationship? How would the ending change?

DRAMATIC STRATEGIES THAT DISMANTLE CULTURAL CONSTRUCTIONS

Several of the following strategies have been borrowed from literary devices of writers claiming to be postmodern. Two authors from whom I have borrowed several ideas are Hutcheon (1988) and McHale (1988). Combined with the questions and conversations in the first section of this chapter, these strategies provide a vast amount and variety of ways to process, present, and perform texts. In the following section the name of the strategy to be dismantled is in italics. There is a plethora of resources from theater, directing, acting, costuming, set designing, and so forth, that can be modified or changed or inserted to make them compatible with the theories and practices of cultural studies and criticism. Borrow from as many sources as possible to energize your practices and inform your theories. Even classical approaches are valuable to include.

1. *Locating the Modern.* Have the students, in groups of five, improvise a two-minute scenario based on an accumulation of their experiences. The text could be one of a mainstream, status quo, family scene with everyday actions, relationships, and dialogue. Caution the students not to exaggerate, or dishonor their realities. At the end of the scenario, another group of five students would be required to reperform the same scenario. However, the second group is to act against the grain. There are several ways

that this could happen. For example, one family member could be carrying a secret that will dismantle the status quo of the family structure. Another way of acting against the grain is for one member of this scene to change the beginning, middle, or ending of the story that takes the dominant reading of family into the realm of alternative readings or multiple readings. Another way for the second group to dismantle the preferred reading of family is for one of the actors to challenge, while in-role, the power of one of the other family members. Another possible acting against the grain strategy would be for an audience member to reposition one of the powerless characters into a role of power and do so by suggesting to the actor how they might achieve consent to a shift in power through a hegemonic practice or discourse.

2. *Multiple Readings.* Chamber theater is a good way of encouraging multiple readings of a cultural text. For example, one group of students could present a cultural text from everyday experience or from scripted text, a piece of literature, a magazine article, a television show, or film and present a two-minute section of the text. Then other groups (each containing five students) will improvise and perform multiple readings of the original scenario. For example, one group may choose to read and rewrite the gender, or race, or class, or age constructions of the original scenario. Another group may choose to read the original text as a historical construction. Another group may choose to introduce a subtext based on an actor's "subject" representation of inner thought about his or her position in the scenario. Another group may choose to introduce a character who was invisible in the original scenario, but would change the status quo presented in the original scenario.

3. *Resistance.* Present a two-minute scenario taken from an everyday situation in a status quo, institutional context such as family, school, church, office, military, government, hospital, stores, shopping malls, restaurants, immigration offices, student services, university, business, airport, border crossing, or any institutional structure, superstructure, or infrastructure. Present a two-minute original, untouched text. Have the audience select one actor who is going to organize resistance to the status quo of the scenario. What strategies does the actor use that are against the grain? What strategies does the audience suggest? What strategies are hegemonic practices?

4. *Historical Consciousness.* Have the students research a historical character. The character could be a highly recognizable individual such as Napoleon, Churchill, Mao Tse-tung, Gandhi, Catherine the Great, Jesus, Mohammed, Patton, or any other famous, historical figure. Insert the historical figure into a modern-day scene such as family, church service, a government office, or any other institutional context. Based on how that figure influenced, terrorized, or changed the history of the world, how would they act, what discourse would they use, how would they influence and/or change life in a modern scenario? How would others resist?

5. *Invisible Histories.* Have the students brainstorm what historical events they have studied in school. Present a report on one of the events listed as a media report by an actor in-role. After the report, have the students in-role as people from different races, gender, sexualities, age, class, physical differences, or other cultural constructions who were present at the time of the historical event, but whose stories were not heard in the report. Have them challenge the media report based on the fact that the original report did not include their truths, knowledge, facts, values, and so forth. In other words, they are persons whose histories have not been told but were present at the historical event selected.

6. *The Halved Soul.* Have the students brainstorm stories from their past that have been told to them by family, community, church, school, literature, or other contexts. The range of stories should reveal a plethora of local, historical, and traditional mythology. For example, one could be the story of Adam and Eve. Have the characters reenact the mythological story. However, at certain points during the reenactment, a third character will stop the action and challenge the cultural constructions that are usually taken for granted or assumed that that is the way life is to be or is natural by taking one of the characters aside and pointing out to them that he or she is powerless, excluded, and that this does not have to be so. Pintar (1992) does this in her book *The Halved Soul.* Adam and Eve are in the Garden of Eden. They are carrying out the actions and conversations in a manner true to the traditional telling of the myth. Lillith, a biblical character who was unaccepting of the traditional cultural constructions of the time, interrupts the Adam and Eve conversation to point out how Eve is being dominated and rendered powerless by accepting Adam's or biblical mythology.

7. *Hero Shifting.* Have the students in groups of five improvise or present from a scripted text a two-minute scenario in which there is a hero. After the scenario, decide what it was that made the character a hero. Have other groups present the same scenario, but this time make a minor character the hero. In other words, if the original hero was so because of rescue or working at the center of the cultural constructions or because of gender, race, age, or because of the knowledge, values, beliefs, mainstream physical attributes, or other mainstream attributes, change those qualities that would make him or her nonmainstream yet still a hero. What should be noted here is that heroes are not traditionally mainstream, but embodied stereotypes. The idea of this strategy is to value marginal attributes to place the possessor in a different position of agency.

8. *Losing Privilege.* Present a scenario in which one or more of the characters moves to a position of marginalization, and re-act how he/she/they would think and act in this new position. This strategy is borrowed from Sue Townsend's (1993), *The Queen and I,* in which the Queen and her family have to move to the projects or a low-rent government-subsidized housing area. For example, Prince Charming and Cinderella lose their wealth, and, thus, have to live on public assistance—a reconstruction of privilege.

9. *Ludic Nature.* Present a mainstream, institutional scenario. Through the strategies of exaggeration, parody, or irony, reveal the ludic nature of the power relationships within the scenario.

10. *Postmodern Spies.* Have a group of five students present a modern-day scenario. Have other students in-role as marginalized people based on gender, race, sexual orientation, class, knowledge, age, and so forth, and interrupt the scenario to reveal and point out to the mainstream characters how their thoughts and actions are part of the crisis of modernity, modernization, and modernism. The characters who interrupt should also think of themselves as from a postmodern, poststructural, postcolonial world. How would they suggest to the modern-day characters how to change their thoughts, actions, knowledge, values, institutions, structures, and other cultural constructions that would move the scenario and the characters into a postmodern world?

11. *Underground Reports.* Have the students bring in newspaper or magazine articles on modern-day people, characters, events, reports, situations, or issues. Based on one of the articles, have a

group of students go in-role to be reporters/writers that interviewed or were present at the time at which the event in the article occurred. Another group of students will be the characters involved in the article. Another group of students will be in-role as reporters of an underground newspaper. This latter group will report such things as: What are the misrepresentations? the gendered truths? the racial truths? the gendered knowledge? the racial knowledge? and so forth, that would not be allowed in the original, mainstream newspaper article.

12. *Recurring Dreams.* Both myth and dream can explore the archaic and the repressed, as a way of unsettling the illusion of subjective autonomy and conscious control and as a way of moving beyond the categories of the rational and the knowable toward a site of creative, multiple subjectivity. Have a group of students create a scenario from mainstream, modern life. Upon completion of the scenario, one of the characters visits a counseling or therapist's office. The office has two therapists: One has been informed by modern theories; the other has been informed by postmodern, poststructural, and postcolonial theories. In therapy, the character reveals how he or she has recurring dreams of oppression, marginalization, powerlessness, and so forth. What suggestions and discourse would each of the two therapists apply?

13. *Symbolic Negotiations.* Have a group of five students present an everyday scenario using any cultural text. Encourage the students to explore a variety of cultural contexts ranging from family to friends to school or other institutional settings. Two of the characters in the scenario must have a problematic relationship. As the scene unfolds, and the problematic relationship is revealed, it should do so mainly through an absence of linguistic, social, or cultural constructions unavailable to one of the characters; it should not fit the mainstream discourse or the social or cultural constructions of the other character. As the two characters attempt symbolic negotiation, have other characters in-role attempt to provide multiple and alternative symbolic negotiations. In other words, how can the actors in a problematic situation use the theories of hegemony to move the two characters to moments of consent without either gaining or losing power?

14. *Quest for the Folk.* Have the students bring in photographs (family or historical) from the past. Take one of the photographs and

have a group of students create a scenario of that photograph at the time it was taken. For example, *Quest for the Folk* (1994) uses a photograph of two Nova Scotia fishing "folk" and provides a poststructural reading. The author demonstrates how the tourist industry created a notion of Nova Scotians as "folk" as a cultural construction that is nonexistent; a misrepresentation, and a strategy to prevent Nova Scotians from moving into the modern world. From the photograph, tourists are led to believe that these "folk" are quaint, simple, fishing people, and that if they visit Nova Scotia, they will see that life in the 1990s is as it was two hundred years ago. So as the students in-role present the scenario of the photograph, the audience in-role as tourist guides present a romantic notion of the past. The students in the photograph scenario of the past step into the discourse and challenge the tour guides of the modern world. An additional strategy here would incorporate anthropologists who would dismantle the cultural constructions of the photograph based on their information of postmodern, poststructural, and postcolonial theories.

15. *Carnivalesque.* Bakhtin (see Holquist, 1990) uses the metaphor of carnival to develop his theory of multiple discourses of the text. He likens multiple readings of a text to the ancient, medieval market town square show (that is similar to the current presentations at local markets or docksides by a variety of professional busker acts). Borrowing Bakhtin's metaphor, have the students in-role at a carnival or as buskers challenge the status quo or culturally constructed attitudes of the audience. For example, Derek Stevens from Ripon, England, had his students in his course Cultural Studies through Theater set up the drama studio as a carnival. The many booths dealt with issues of power and marginalization, such as the elderly, homeless, homosexuals, physically different, and so forth. The audience, students from other classes, visited the booths expecting carnival activities but were met with subtexts of interpretation. One example used an effigy where the audience was invited to use sponge bats to bash the effigy and win a prize if they could knock it over. However, around the effigy were newspaper clippings and other symbolic representations of homosexual culture. It was evident that the effigy represented a homosexual person. What was frightening about the presentation was that several audience participants took delight in "gay bashing."

16. *Fracturing Organic Unity.* Modern constructions seem to work at organic unity. However, in the postmodern, poststructural world, drama will consist of juxtapositions and interruptions that dismantle conventional knowledge, values, and structures. This strategy should force both the actors and the audience into critical speculation. This is not revolutionary thinking, but an area of thinking that moves us toward the postmodern. Students in the dramatic arts informed by contemporary theories should be able to develop a repertoire of dramatic strategies that fracture assumed organic unity of modern thought. Therefore, any performance or presentation, both improvised and scripted, should include interruptions and juxtapositions by dramatic devices such as interruptions of character development, plot sequence, and, of course, dialogue/discourse.

17. *Radical Remembrances.* Agger (1990) states that remembrance is a radical response to memory. Although we must never forget the past, dramatic strategies in the postmodern era would act against the grain of those memories, and act as a rebellious imagination and give us the power to resist the manipulation of history. Students in the dramatic arts can provide scenarios of personal and public memories, again from both improvised and scripted material; however, these memories must challenge, question, or change the ideas, knowledge, values, and events as they were thought to have occurred through our memories. One strategy might be to include an in-role character with radical thoughts into the context of the memory being represented through the scenario.

18. *Cultural Critics.* Students could take a familiar story (such as a fairy tale) and have the characters, plot, event, or setting engaged in critical theory issues as introduced in the previous chapters.

19. *Schizophrenic Interpretations.* Schizophrenia, according to Lacan (1977), is already a plurality of interpretations. Develop a narrator with schizophrenic thoughts evolving from multiple memories, confused memories, fractured memories, incomplete memories, or multiple personality, multiple knowledge, values, and truths about a cultural construction including personal (e.g., family or friends) or a public institution (e.g., school, church, military, media). Have the narrator inserted into the dramatic text with no single consistent subjectivity, history, and so forth. The intent is poststructural in that life is a contingency of

knowledge, truths, and structures and the plurality of the schizo-phrenia's interpretations are a challenge to single, fixed, ab-solute meaning, discourse, and so on.

20. *Contradicting Staticity.* Contemporary theories challenge the fixity and staticity of the modern world. Develop a series of sce-narios based on the same context and content, for example, a hospital emergency room. Divide the students into groups of five, and present each group with the same scenario; however, each group in sequence is to reenact the previous scenario by showing the contradictions in truths, knowledge, values, and so forth, that existed or were exclusive.

21. *Contradictory Texts.* Contemporary theories generally tend to claim that there is no closed coherent or noncontradictory world or subjectivity. Students, in whatever dramatic art is being re-hearsed, presented, or performed, should prevent any totalizing concepts of the world or subjectivity. The actors must prevent the audience from being able to find or take any one subject's position. The audience through the actors' strategies should be asked to confront and recognize contradictions within the text being shown.

22. *Conferring Subjectivity.* Each of us is constructed by history and a series of totalizing discourses that tend to inscribe us as uni-fied, coherent subjects (e.g., female neurotic, physically dis-abled, homosexual, Oriental, white, old, middle class, and the plethora of other culturally constructed discourses). Subjectivity as fixed is a modern construction. In a postcontemporary world, there are multiple ways to confer subjectivity and, thus, multiple subjectivities within a "subject" construction (e.g., family, his-tory, mythology, school, media, literature, science). Have the students bring in samples of a subjectivity (e.g., unwed women/ mothers, a racial group, the elderly, and so forth) constructed through oral, printed, and visual discourses collected from liter-ature, journals, magazines, television, films, diaries, newspa-pers, works of art, scripted dramatic texts, or other resources. Have the students insert these different discourses into an impro-vised or already scripted text that focuses on the construction of subjectivity.

23. *Manual on Resistance.* The purpose of this strategy is to have the actors or the audience in-role gain an ideological awareness of the political, social, and linguistic structures embedded within a

constructed text. Have a group of students present an improvised scenario or section of a scripted text or dramatic arts' performance (from mime to theater to clowning to buskering), especially a text that is about an obvious cultural group based on, for example, gender, race, class, sexuality, age, and so on. After the presentation, the audience in-role is to present a manual (a "how-to" book) to the actors on possible ways to resist, without violence, the traditional status quo, mainstream cultural construction that has been imposed hegemonically upon them by political, social, and linguistic structures. Then have the actors re-present or reperform the text. Were they able to incorporate resistances into the ideological experience? In all strategies, actors and intervenors should always stay in-role even when reflecting on or discussing actions of the scenario.

24. *Constructed Reality.* Whose reality is being represented? Whatever the dramatic art and content that is being performed, students of cultural criticism would dismantle the text by asking whose reality is being represented and what hegemonic practices were in place to construct a reality to which so many people consent.

25. *We Interrupt This Program.* On day one of a dramatic arts session, have the students decide upon an issue, a historical or contemporary event, or any other topic they decide they would like to explore and dismantle. Have one of the groups of students present a scenario focusing on their chosen topic. For homework, the students are to collect and bring in for the next session newspaper clippings, posters, captions, songs, popular sayings, advertisements, cliches, or other formats that are drawn from popular culture and related to the chosen topic. The original scenario is presented; however, the other students interrupt at different points with a reading of their gathered material. The purpose of this strategy is to use art as a forum for students to rehearse speaking out politically.

26. *Intertexual Parody.* In Hutcheon (1988, p. 225), the author talks about *Ragtime* (Doctorow, 1975), having Freud and Jung ride through the Coney Island Tunnel of Love. She claims that this is a postmodern mingling of the historical and the self-reflexive—a type of intertextual parody. The conversation between the two characters of similar areas of knowledge but with different theories would be a strategy to insert in a dramatic text. The list of

symbolically similar but historically different characters and points of view is endless.

27. *Different Realities.* The postmodern consciousness focuses on shifting and changing the dominant cultural constructions, exploiting the possibilities of the plurality of worlds, and transgressing the boundaries between worlds (McHale, 1989)—worlds of knowledge, truths, values, gender, race, class, age, and so on. With this in mind, students should be constantly reminded that the purpose of any dramatic strategy is to match the theoretical essence of contemporary theories. One of the challenges is to dismantle status quo, mainstream knowledge as full of misconceptions and contradictions. There is no one knowledge. After presenting a scenario, the students identify the mainstream knowledge embedded within the dramatic text. After identification, the students either modify, change, or insert new knowledge that changes the dominant knowledge. For example, Native Americans/aboriginal people structure the world quite differently than nonnative people. Collect information on Native Americans' ways of structuring the world. Present a scenario in which this knowledge influences or changes mainstream nonnative knowledge. The same could apply to truths, gender, and so forth.

28. *Inner Thoughts.* Another strategy that involves a common device in theater is the interior monologue in which the speaker reveals his or her inner thoughts to the audience or other characters who eavesdrop. For our purposes, however, the monologue would contain the thoughts and discourse that dismantle mainstream cultural constructions. The inner monologue expresses a frustration with modern life (at least very specific aspects). The inner monologue would also be less directed at self (e.g., to be or not to be) and more directed at the social, political, and ideological world (e.g., to participate or not to participate in changing the world; to resist or not to resist; to consent or not to consent).

29. *Discontinued Thoughts.* Introduce two characters into a scenario who have contrasting minds, one of which is drawn from the fictional world (i.e., literature, film, television, oral and written texts, and any artwork) and the other of which is drawn from the real world (i.e., personal history, newspapers, textbook information, and so forth). The insertion of these two contrasting minds should reveal both a continuity and, more importantly, the discontinuity of our thinking in a contemporary world.

30. *Voyeurism.* Have one group of students present a scenario. Other students are inserted secretly into the scenario in different ways, for example, by hiding behind a curtain, overhearing a conversation at the next table, picking up an extension phone, accessing someone else's electronic mail, hidden cameras, bugging devices. What is seen or overheard is relayed by the voyeur to other characters or the audience using theories of cultural criticism.

31. *Crossing Cultural Borders.* Since modern life has overconceptualized and fixed boundaries between knowledges, truths, gender, race, age, class, and so forth, the purpose of this dramatic strategy is to break down or cross the boundaries/borders between fixed examples of Border crossing could be done through using traditional fairy tales in which there are very fixed notions of gender, race, family, class, and so forth. Using, for example, the Cinderella story, the traditional family, the single-parent family, and the same-sex family could be invited to each other's family gathering.

32. *Border Crossing.* The transgression of boundaries between worlds as a strategy could involve crossing borders by mixing genres, introducing a science fiction element, or crossing time and space zones (such as Columbus discovers America a full century too late).

33. *Heterotopia—Time Travel.* An example of trans-historical crossing of cultural constructions is borrowed from the film/book *The French Lieutenant's Woman* by John Fowles. Because it is set in modern times—yet, one of the characters is an actress playing the same world in a film—we are never sure what historical time we are actually privy to. In crossing these time boundaries, the audience is exposed to the similarity and differences of a multiple range of cultural constructions. McHale (1988) gives other examples, such as the trans-historical party (where members of different historical periods are invited to a party), for example, a public execution in Times Square.

34. *Escape Routes.* Characters are introduced into a scenario of any modern construct because they have escaped from a particular world. The escape could be from any modern institution (e.g., prison, psychiatric hospital, school, university, office, family, sports team, military, detention centers, concentration camps, internment camps, labor camps, political party). The character who has escaped has to explain why, how, and what they plan to

do to join the contemporary theoretical world of cultural studies and criticism (metaphorically speaking).

35. *Being Sane in Insane Places.* This strategy is based on an actual study by Rosenhan (1973) in which a group of psychologically "sane" individuals admitted themselves into a psychiatric hospital on the ground of pretended schizophrenic symptoms. After admittance, they ceased pretending and then proceeded to try to be released from the institution by acting "normally" (as they would if they were not in the institution). They had difficulty getting release from the institution. Create a scenario that takes place in an institutional setting of any kind with its own institutional boundaries including behaviors, actions, thoughts, codes, interactions, and structures. One character must attempt to be released from the institutional life, yet the other characters carry on according to the institutional boundaries. One humorous example is Klinger in the *M*A*S*H* series, who attempts to be released from military service by acting insane and wearing women's clothing.

36. *I've Been Fired Party.* This is based on an actual situation (Cal Dupree). Native Americans who worked for the Department of Indian Affairs in Alaska were fired by the "white" bosses because they disagreed with the bosses or resisted doing work assigned by the bosses because it was not work that was compatible to the way Native Americans think or act. The Native Americans would then throw a party as a way of celebrating their resistance to an institution for Native Americans being run and structured by non-Native people. Extend this strategy to other institutional constructions that are exclusive or contradictory to the people who work there.

37. *Epistemological Quests.* Have the students present an improvised or scripted scenario that is representative of modern-day cultural constructions. Introduce the strategy of the "epistemological quest" (we need to know) through a detective, lawyer, judge, or police officer character. This dramatic device dismantles the knowledge and bridges the gap between appearances and reality, and allows questioning of the reliability of every cultural construction. It is assumed that the epistemological positioning of the character has been informed by theories of cultural studies and criticism.

38. *Human Agency Office.* This strategy uses the notion of an agency office in which the clientele comes to an agency to have them

promote the person or group—for example, modeling agencies, promotion agencies, advertising agencies, and so forth. Create a situation in which a group (in-role as a gender, race, or other cultural construction) are feeling that their voices are not being heard or are being excluded from the mainstream or the center. Have the group present the context in which the silencing or excluding occurred. After this scenario, have the group go to the agency office to present their case. Then the members of the agency must return to the original scenario to confront, resist, and suggest to the silencers/excluders what they must do to hear the voices and include the group.

39. *Swallowed by Nightmares.* Have a group of students in-role as aid workers, or as medical doctors, or as missionaries, or as rescuing pilots, or any other adventurous group organizing a trip to another culture in order to do one of the following: save, convert, rescue, aid, adopt, train, develop, study, intervene, mediate, and so forth. Have another group of students in-role as the culture of the "Other." The adventurous group eventually meets, works, or carries out their agenda among the culture of the "other." Because the "other" either resists or is naive, the adventurous group has difficulty in saving, converting, rescuing, or whatever. Their adventure and intrigue soon turn to nightmares. A caution with this strategy is to keep a sense of honor about the "other" culture without having to position them as unintelligent or uncooperative, or having to reach a point of war.

40. *Tarot Cards.* Have available a set of tarot cards that will be used to redirect mainstream thoughts and structures. Have one group of students present a culturally constructed scenario. While the scenario unfolds, other members of the class turn up a tarot card that will then decide what will happen next to the thoughts and structures of the characters and plot. Calvino (1977) uses this strategy to fracture our notions of literary genre. As he writes, each chapter is based on the turning up of a tarot card, and developing a storyline around that card. The next chapter is the next tarot card and so on.

41. *Fantastic Confrontations.* Have one group of five students present a brief scenario representing a cultural context with a situation of confrontation or resistance. One or more members of the audience interrupts the confrontation or resistance by moving into the scenario in-role as a creature of the fantastic, for example,

dragons, sphinxes, gargoyles, phoenixes, griffins, and so forth. The resistance of normality now is confronting the supernatural or extraordinary that exaggerates the resistances and confrontations of everyday life to raise them from the ordinary to the extraordinary. The result should be an indication of the struggle of the ordinary individual/subjects to confront or resist the ruling, dominant superpowers. It moves the ordinary subject into an agent for change.

42. *Group-Reflexive Journals.* As a scenario on a marginal, invisible, or silenced group of subjects is presented (e.g., homeless, unwed mothers, environmentalists, fisher people), have a critical theorist reflect in a journal on the action of the scenario. The writing should be self-reflexive and indicate how his or her theories, borrowed from cultural studies and criticisms, have or have not influenced or changed the human condition represented by the brief scenario.

43. *Postcolonial Culture,* Present a scenario that would be occurring in a colonized culture. The colonization could be recent or historically distant, could be economic, political, military, or intellectual colonization. Present it as the first stage of colonization in which the colonized take on the discourse and behaviors of the colonizer. Then present the second stage of colonialism in which the colonized resist through discourse and behavior the culture of the imperial power. Present the third scenario in which the colonized have mixed the discourse and behavior of the colonizers with their own. Have fictional colonizers introduced into a scenario (e.g., Columbus, Robinson Caruso, pirates, guerillas, Walt Disney characters, and so forth).

44. *Exiles.* Since the postcolonial is concerned with place, displacement, and relationships with the colonizer, colonized populations are constantly in a state of exile from their own cultural roots, whether they stay within the colony, escape, or leave on their own. Perform a section of a text about or by a colonized culture (remember to expand the notion of colonization to other metaphors such as seduction by money, gender, race). Insert an exile or expatriate into the text and have him or her intervene in the structures, discourses, relationships, and other symbolic constructions. Through the insertion into the context, exiles or expatriates would automatically be deconstructing and challenging the colonized text.

45. *Imaginative Escapes.* Similar to exercise #44, cultures must be liberated from the destructive dialectic of history and entrapped memories. Imagination, as Wilson Harris (1985) claims, is the key. Intervene or change the historical imagination of the dominant constructs by introducing a character who has escaped colonialism and history.

46. *Polyglossic Cultures.* If there are a mixture of dialects and languages among the students in a dramatic arts class, perform a traditional, monolinguistic text. However, speakers of different dialects and languages will perform their parts with a mixture of the dominant language and their own. Translation of words or phrases into the dominant language (for example, non-English into English) is not allowed in this strategy.

47. *Subcultures as Negations.* Subcultures, especially those in the music industry, stress refusal, resistance, revolt, and neglect celebration, confirmation, and community. Texts, whether improvised or scripted, are to be rewritten from the perspective of a subculture that negates the status quo world.

48. *War of Positions.* Create five or six different scenarios borrowed from literature or films/television/media that re-create a context of relationships in or by spy organizations. Creating a "war of positions," have one group spy on another group and then report back with the exclusions and misrepresentations of family, school, court, church, press, and so forth. Ask who and what is glorified, is demoted or dismissed, and, as well, what soundtracks, clothing, fashion, interior design dominates. This strategy should examine the revealing minority roles of women, children, Third World, people of color, and the elderly (McHale, 1989, p. 7).

49. *Deconstructing Romance.* McHale (1989) talks about popular romance that confirms or determines women's desires as popular romance—monogamous, heterosexual marriage—while "masculine romances" (Westerns or stories, thrillers, spy novels, detective stories, and boys' adventures) pay attention to male solidarity and camaraderie (pp. 78, 79). Dismantle mainstream romances through dramatic strategies.

50. *Worlds Next Door.* One way to challenge the mainstream is through split-staging such as Fuentes's strategy of a young historian occupying the rear of an aged woman's suburban house, and the ghost of a younger self of a woman. As the drama

unfolds, whose discourse world, knowledge, race, history, and so forth, becomes dominant? Try other split-staging contexts based on class, race, physical, intellectual, and so on.

51. *Crucial Issues.* Represent part of the story in which a subject must deal with a critical issue, for example, have some of the subjects protest against a position because a person is of a marginalized gender, race, and so forth. How do you deal with this problem? Demonstrate the other stereotypical beliefs, values, and attitudes. Introduce a conversational response that has members become aware of their oppressive and devaluing responses to the excluded subject. What attitudes, values, and opinions toward these activities are being formulated? How may a lack of participation or social support oppress the subject? Where, when, and how does the oppressed subject lose/gain agency? Introduce a character who changes the direction of oppression.

52. *Troping.* Tropes are metaphors that create images, for example, "I'm having a blonde day" (it means that a person is feeling stupid or dumb because the metaphor is "blondes are dumb"). (Thanks to Lissa Paul at UNB for the example.) In this trope, two images are put together that are oppressive or exclusionary. Collect other tropes that privilege one person or group over another by making connections between the privileged and the oppressed. Introduce these into everyday scenarios. Observe how they position the users.

53. *Juxtapositioning of Popular Culture and Reality.* Auslander (1992) talks about the example of juxtapositioning a scene from the *Killing Fields,* followed by an advertisement for breakfast cereal. Another example is the programs on aid to the Third World that show hungry and starving children followed by a commercial for fast food. Use these as examples to create your own cultural contexts that juxtaposition reality with oppositions from popular culture.

54. *Sterilized Solutions.* Auslander (1992) tells how the women in a shampoo factory were requested to have themselves sterilized (so they cannot have children) because of the toxic waste in the shampoo. Native women along the Rocky Mountains were sterilized by government officials in order to prevent them having more children and repeating the cycle of poverty. Create scenarios in which solutions to problems are ridiculous, but hegemonic (remember in both cases women were told that they could keep their jobs or live better if they did not have children).

55. *Spectacle Managers.* Politicians and dictators can be known as "spectacle managers," where they create politics of ecstasy. An example is Hitler, who managed to organize a group of "spectacle managers" to sell his propaganda. Nowadays, "spectacle organizers" create hegemony through the organization of "spectacles." Take an everyday occurrence or situation and hire a "spectacle manager" to move the ordinary into the extraordinary. Actual, everyday examples exist that move, over time, from an extraordinary into an ordinary, hegemonic state (for example, homelessness, poverty, violence, abuse, crime, youth suicide, to name just a few). Spectacle managers disturb the ordinary and enlighten the crisis by raising it to the extraordinary. One drama group used the game show persona, hype, discourse, and prize granting as a spectacle manager for a homeless character. At first the scenario was light and humorous. As the "spectacle managers" continued, an air of tension and discomfort developed and in the final moments of the scenario the "spectacle managers" froze before awarding the homeless character the prize of a microwave. The silence of the audience and the actors indicated the shock of homelessness. Another group used the strategy of spectacle managers to present a scenario of a battered woman. The group acted as "spectacle managers" of a baseball team that included the unidentified battered woman. After a series of "spectacles" including a charade-type mime scene of bat, batting, batter, battered—a pause—then the team and audience revelation of a "battered" woman.

Bibliography

Adam, I., and Tiffin, H. (eds.). (1990). *Past the Last Post: Theorizing Post-Colonialism and Post-Modernism.* Calgary, Alberta: University of Calgary Press.

Adamson, W.L. (1980). *Hegemony and Revolution—A Study of Antonio Gramsci's Political and Cultural Theory.* Berkeley: University of California Press.

Agger, B. (1990). *The Decline of Discourse: Reading, Writing, and Resistance in Postmodern Capitalism.* New York: Falmer Press.

Agger, B. (1991). *A Critical Theory of Public Life: Knowledge, Discourse and Politics in an Age of Decline.* London: Falmer Press.

Agger, B. (1992). *Cultural Studies as Critical Theory.* London: Falmer Press.

Albert, L.V. (1985). *Cut.* Toronto: Playwrights Union of Canada.

Althusser, L. (1972). *Politics and History: Montesquien, Rousseau, Hegel, and Marx.* London: National Library Books.

Ashcroft, B., Griffiths, G., and Tiffin, H. (eds.). (1989). *Empire Writes Back: Theory and Practice in Post-Colonial Literatures.* London: Routledge.

Aston, E. (1995). *An Introduction to Feminism and Theatre.* New York: Routledge.

Auslander, P. (1992). *Presence and Resistance: Postmodernism and Cultural Politics in Contemporary American Performance.* Ann Arbor: University of Michigan Press.

Barker, F. (1993). *The Culture of Violence: Essays on Tragedy and History.* Manchester, England: Manchester University Press.

Barthes, R. (1986). *The Rustle of Language.* New York: Hill and Wang.

Baudrillard, J. (1988). *Jean Baudrillard: Selected Writings.* Cambridge, England: Polity Press.

Bear, N. Personal communication. (1994). Fredericton: University of New Brunswick.

Becker, H., and McCall, M. M. (1988). *Symbolic Interaction and Cultural Studies*. Chicago: University of Chicago Press.

Benhabib, S. (1992). *Situating the Self—Gender, Community, and Postmodernism in Contemporary Ethics*. Cambridge, England: Polity Press.

Berry, C. (1993). *Voice and the Actor*. U.K.: Virgin.

Berry, K. S. (1989). *Mythically-Based Curriculum: A Passion for the Possible*. Unpublished Ph.D. dissertation. Edmonton: University of Alberta.

Birringer, J. (1991). *Theatre, Theory, Postmodernism*. Bloomington: Indiana University Press.

Blundell, V., Shepherd, J., and Taylor, I. (eds.). (1993). *Relocating Cultural Studies: Developments in Theory and Research*. London: Routledge.

Boal, A. (1985). *Theatre of the Oppressed*. New York: Theatre Communications Group.

Bocock, R. (1986). *Hegemony*. New York: Tavistock.

Bogg, C. (1976). *Gramsci's Marxism*. London: Pluto Press.

Bolton, G. (1979). *Towards a Theory of Drama in Education*. London: Longman.

Booth, D.W., and Lundy, C. J. (1985). *Improvisation: Learning through Drama*.

Boyne, R., and Rattansi, A. (1990). *Postmodernism and Society*. New York: Macmillan.

Brooker, P. (1992). *Modernism—Postmodernism*. New York: Longman.

Butler, J. (1993). *Bodies That Matter: On the Discursive Limits of Sex*. New York: Routledge.

Calvino, I. (1977). *The Castle of Crossed Destinies*. New York: Harcourt Brace Jovanovich.

Caputo, J.D. (1987). *Radical Hermeneutics: Repetition, Deconstruction and the Hermeneutics Project*. Indianapolis: Indiana University Press.

Crichlow, W., and McCarthy, C. (eds.). *Cultural Studies: Toni Morrison and the Curriculum*. Special Issue, May 1995.

Denzin, N. (1991). *Images of Postmodern Society: Social Theory and Contemporary Cinema*. London: Sage.

Denzin, N. K. (1992). *Symbolic Interactionism and Cultural Studies: The Politics of Interpretation*. Oxford, England: Blackwell.

Dolan, J. (1993). *Presence and Desire: Essays on Gender, Sexuality, Performance*. Ann Arbor: University of Michigan Press.

Doyle, C. (1993). *Raising Curtains on Education: Drama as a Site for Critical Pedagogy*. Toronto: Ontario Institute for Studies in Education.

Eagan, K. (1990). *Romantic Understanding: The Development of Rationality and Imagination, Ages 8–15*. New York: Routledge.

Eliade, M. (1964). *Shamanism: Archaic Techniques of Ecstasy.* Princeton: Princeton University Press.

Eyre, L. (1994). Personal communication. Fredericton: University of New Brunswick.

Femia, J. V. (1981). *Gramsci's Political Thought—Hegemony, Consciousness, and the Revolutionary Process.* Oxford, England: Clarendon Press.

Fontana, B. (1993). *Hegemony and Power—On the Relation between Gramsci and Machiavelli.* Minneapolis: University of Minnesota Press.

Foucault, M. (1972). *Power/Knowledge: Selected Interviews and Other Writings, 1972–1977.* New York: Pantheon.

Foucault, M. (1977). *Language, Counter-Memory, Practice.* Oxford, England: Blackwell.

Fowles, John. (1969). *The French Lieutenant's Woman.* Boston: Little, Brown.

Freire, P. (1994). *Pedagogy of Hope: Reliving Pedagogy of the Oppressed.* New York: Harcourt Brace Jovanovich.

Fuentes, C. (1975). *Terra Nostra.* New York: Penguin Books.

Gadamer, H-G. (1982). *Truth and Method.* New York: Crossroad Publishing.

Gamble, A. (1988). *The Free Economy and the Strong State: The Politics of Thatcherism.* London: Macmillan.

Gates, H. L., Jr. (1995). "Annals of Race—Thirteen Ways of Looking at a Black Man." *New Yorker Magazine* (Oct. 23, 1995).

Giroux, H. A. (1991). *Postmodernism, Feminism, and Cultural Politics—Redrawing Educational Boundaries.* New York: State University of New York Press.

Giroux, H. (1992). *Border Crossings.* New York: Routledge.

Golding, S. (1992). *Gramsci's Democratic Theory—Contribution to a Post-Liberal Democracy.* Toronto: University of Toronto Press.

Goodman, L. (1993). *Contemporary Feminist Theatres: To Each Her Own.* London: Routledge.

Gramsci, A. (1973). *Letters from Prison.* New York: Harper & Row.

Grossberg, L. (1992). *We Gotta Get Out of This Place: Popular Conservatism and Postmodern Culture.* New York: Routledge.

Habermas, J. (1984). *The Theory of Communicative Action: Volume One—Reason and the Rationalization of Society.* Boston: Beacon Press.

Harris, Whiteness. (1985). *The Guyana Quartet.* Boston: Faber and Faber.

Heidegger, M. (1977). *Basic Writings.* New York: Harper & Row.

Hilton, J. (1993). *New Directions in Theatre.* London: Macmillan.

Holub, R. (1992). *Antonio Gramsci—Beyond Marxism and Postmodernism.* New York: Routledge.

Holquist, M. (1990). *Dialogism: Bakhtin and His World.* New York: Routledge.

hooks, b. (1990). *Yearning: Race, Gender, and Cultural Politics.* Toronto: Between the Lines.

Hutcheon, L. (1988). *The Poetics of Postmodernism: History, Theory, Fiction.* New York: Routledge.

Hutcheon, L. (1989). *The Politics of Postmodernism.* New York: Routledge.

Husserl, E. (1964). *The Idea of Phenomenology.* The Hague: Martimus Nighoff.

Jenks, C. (1993). *Cultural Reproduction.* New York: Routledge.

Kellner, D., and Best, S. (1991). *Postmodern Theories—Critical Interrogations.* New York: Guilford Press.

Kelly, U. (1993). *Marketing Place: Cultural Politics, Regionalism and Reading.* Halifax, Nova Scotia: Fernwood.

Kershaw, B. (1992). *The Politics of Performance: Radical Theatre as Cultural Intervention.* London: Routledge.

Kuhn, T. S. (1970). *The Structure of Scientific Revolutions.* Chicago: University of Chicago Press.

Lacan, J. (1977). *Ecrits: A Selection.* New York: Norton.

Lash, S. (1989). *Sociology of Postmodernism.* New York: Routledge.

Lather, P. (1991). *Getting Smart: Feminist Research and Pedagogy within the Postmodern.* New York: Routledge.

Leitch, V. B. (1992). *Cultural Criticism, Literary Theory, Poststructuralism.* New York: Columbia University Press.

Lyotard, F. (1989). *The Postmodern Condition: A Report on Knowledge.* Minneapolis: University of Minnesota Press.

Marshall, B. K. (1992). *Teaching the Postmodern: Fiction and Theory.* New York: Routledge.

McHale, B. (1989). *Postmodernist Fiction.* New York: Routledge.

McKay, I. (1994). *The Quest of the Folk: Antimodernism and Cultural Selection in Twentieth Century Nova Scotia.* Montreal: McGill-Queen's University Press.

Merleau-Ponty, M. (1962). *Phenomenology of Perception.* London: Routledge and Kegan.

Miller, J. (1990). *Seductions: Studies in Reading and Culture.* London: Virago.

Milner, A. (1994). *Contemporary Cultural Theory: An Introduction.* London: UCL Press.

Morrison, T. (1992) *Playing in the Dark: Whiteness in the Literary Imagination.* Toronto: Random House of Canada Limited.

Musashi, M. (1982). *A Book of Five Rings.* New York: Overlook Press.

Myrsiades, K., and Myrsiades, L. S. (eds.). (1994). *Margins in the Classroom: Teaching Literature.* Minneapolis: University of Minnesota Press.

Neelands, J., and Goode, T. (eds.). (1991) Structuring Drama Work: A Handbook of Available Forms in Theatre and Drama. Boston, Mass.: Cambridge University Press.

Neuman, S., and Stephenson, G. (1993). *Re-Imagining Woman.* Toronto: University of Toronto Press.

Nichols, T. (1995). Personal communication. Fredericton: University of New Brunswick.

Nietzsche, F. (1957). *The Use and Abuse of History.* Indianapolis: Bobbs and Merill.

O'Neill, C. (1984). *The Collected Writings of Dorothy Heathcote.* London: Hutchinson.

O'Neill, C., and Lambert, A. (1982). *Structures—A Practical Handbook for Teachers.* London: Hutchinson.

O'Neill, C., Lambert, A., Linnell, R., and Wan-Wood, J. (1976). *Drama Guidelines.* London: London Drama.

Pefanis, J. (1991). *Heterology and the Postmodern.* Durham, NC: Duke University Press.

Philippi, D. (1982). *Songs of Gods, Songs of Human: The Epic Tradition of the Ainu.* San Francisco: Northpoint Press.

Pintar, J. (1992). *The Halved Soul.* London: Pandora Press.

Probyn, E. (1993). *Sexing the Self: Gendered Positions in Cultural Studies.* New York: Routledge.

Rodenburg, P. (1993). *The Need For Words: Voice and the Text.* London: Methuen Drama.

Rorty, R. (1989). *Contingency, Irony, and Solidarity.* New York: Cambridge University Press.

Rosenhan, D. L. (1973). "On Being Sane in Insane Places." *Science* (Jan. 19, 1973, p. 250).

Said, E.W. (1978). *Orientalism.* New York: Pantheon Books.

Said, E.W. (1993). *Culture and Imperialism.* New York: Knopf.

Salamini, L. (1981). *The Sociology of Political Praxis—An Introduction to Gramsci's Theory.* New York: Routledge.

Sarup, M. (1993). *An Introductory Guide to Post-Structuralism and Post-Modernism.* Toronto: Harvester, Wheatsheaf.

Sassoon, A. S. (ed.). (1983). *Approaches to Gramsci.* London: Writers and Readers Publishing Cooperative Society.

Schon, D. (1983). *The Reflective Practioner: How Professionals Think in Action.* New York: Basic Books.

Selden, R. (1993). *A Reader's Guide to Contemporary Literary Theory.* Lexington: University Press of Kentucky.

Shannon, P. (1990). *The Struggle to Continue: Progressive Reading Instruction in the United States.* Portsmouth: Heinemann.

Shor, I., and Freire, P. (1987). *A Pedagogy for Liberation: Dialogues on Transforming Education.* South Hadley, Mass.: Bergin and Garvey.

Simon, R. (1982). *Gramsci's Political Thought—An Introduction.* London: Lawrence & Wishart Publishers.

Steiner, G. (1982). *Language and Silence: Essays on Language, Literature and the Inhuman.* New York: Atheneum.

Storey, J. (1993). *An Introductory Guide to Cultural Theory and Popular Culture.* New York: Harvester, Wheatsheaf.

Thwaites, D. L., and Mules, W. (1994). *Tools for Cultural Studies: An Introduction.* Melbourne: Macmillan Education.

Townsend, S. (1993). *The Queen and I.* U.K.: Mandarin.

Usher, R., and Edwards, R. (1994). *Postmodernism and Education.* New York: Routledge.

Van Manen, M. (1991). *The Tact of Teaching: The Meaning of Pedagogical Thoughtfulness.* London, Ontario: Althouse Press.

Wagner, B. (1976). *Drama as a Learning Medium.* Evanston: National Education Association.

Wa Thiong'o, N. (1986). *Decolonising the Mind: The Politics of Language in African Literature.* Nairobi: Heinemann.

Watkins, B. (1981). *Drama and Education.* London: Batsford.

Watson, J. D. (1968). *The Double Helix.* New York: Atheneum.

Watson, L. (1976). *Gifts of Unknown Things.* Kent, England: Hodder and Stoughton Limited.

White, S. (1991). *Political Theory and Postmodernism.* Cambridge, England: Cambridge University Press.

White, S. K. (1978). *Tropics of Discourse.* Baltimore: Johns Hopkins University Press.

Williams, P. , and Williams, L. (eds.). (1993). *Colonial Discourse and Post-Colonial Theory: A Reader.* New York: Harvester, Wheatsheaf.

Wiseman, M. B. (1989). *The Ecstasies of Roland Barthes.* New York: Routledge.

Witkin, R. W. (1974). *The Intelligence of Feeling.* London: Heinemann.

Wright, E. (1989). *Postmodern Brecht: A Re-Presentation.* London: Routledge.

Zavarzadeh, M., and Morton, D. (1994). *Theory As Resistance—Politics and Culture after (Post)Structuralism.* New York: Guilford Press.

Index

About the Author

Kathleen S. Berry is a Professor of Education in Cultural Studies, Drama, and Literacy at the University of New Brunswick, Fredericton, Canada. Her work is centered on educational worlds and the impact of cultural studies and criticism on theories and practices in pedagogy, drama, and multi-literacies. She has written articles, chapters, and books related to her areas of study, including *Three Approaches to Literacy: A Handbook for Teachers* (University of New Brunswick). Chapters are included in *13 Questions: Reframing Education* (Lang); *Unauthorized Methods* (Routledge); *Students as Researchers* (Falmer); *Dismantling White Privilege* (Lang); and *The Postformal Reader* (Garland), edited by Joe Kincheloe and Shirley Steinberg. In process are chapters on Gardner's multiple intelligences; educational psychology's pedacide; whiteness in Canada; and a book on postformalist pedagogies and literacies.